To Emery,
   Thank you my friend for your input and advice during the editing phase of this book.

   John R. Richardson

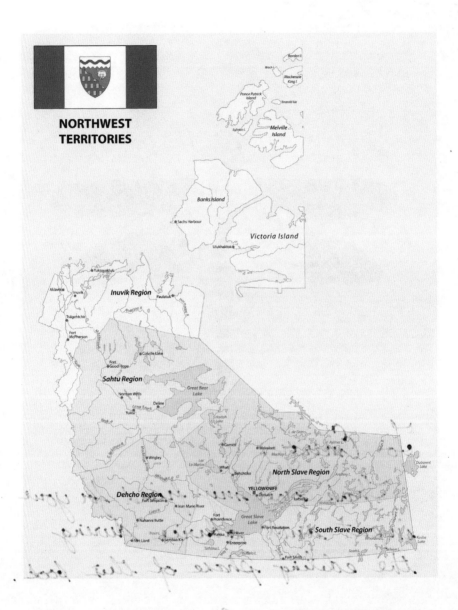

PERSEVERANCE

One Month Canoeing the Mackenzie River

John R. Richardson

 FriesenPress

Suite 300 - 990 Fort St
Victoria, BC, V8V 3K2
Canada

www.friesenpress.com

Copyright © 2020 by John R. Richardson
First Edition — 2020

All rights reserved.

No part of this publication may be reproduced in any form, or by any means, electronic or mechanical, including photocopying, recording, or any information browsing, storage, or retrieval system, without permission in writing from FriesenPress.

ISBN
978-1-5255-7408-5 (Hardcover)
978-1-5255-7409-2 (Paperback)
978-1-5255-7410-8 (eBook)

1. BIOGRAPHY & AUTOBIOGRAPHY, PERSONAL MEMOIRS

Distributed to the trade by The Ingram Book Company

Disclaimer: The author and publisher believe this book may be helpful to others planning or preparing for a similar river expedition, but it must be understood that this journey took place in 2006, and much has changed since then. The Mackenzie River has changed course—as rivers do every year—equipment has been modified, and services have likely changed. The author and publisher do not assume and hereby disclaim any liability to any party for any loss of property, loss of life, damage to property, injury, or disruption caused by errors or omissions, whether such errors or omissions result from negligence, accident, or any other cause.

Table of Contents

Introduction 1
Acknowledgments 6
    On the Way 8
    The Day Before the Beginning 16
    Departure 20
    Big Fish and High Water 25
    Jean Marie River 31
    Fort Simpson 34
    Wrigley Ferry 39
    Nahanni River 42
    Willowlake River 46
    Wrigley 50
    Johnson River 55
    Redstone River 59
    South of Seagull Island 64
    Halfway Island 80
    One Mile South of Prohibition Creek 85
    Norman Wells 88
    Canada Day 94
    Uncle Wilfred 97
    Sans Sault Rapids 100
    The Ramparts 105
    Crossing the Arctic Circle 110
    A Better Day 114
    Little Chicago 134
    Travaillant River 138
    Fatigue 142
    Tsiigehtchic 145
    Jackfish Creek Cabin 150
    To Inuvik 157
    Exploring Inuvik 163
    Tuktoyaktuk 168
    Leaving the Arctic 183
Author's Notes 187
Appendix A: Mackenzie River Mile Guide 189

To Sue, my wife of more than fifty-two years, who has consistently provided me with support, shown great patience, modeled perseverance, and given me enduring love.

Introduction

"By failing to prepare, you are preparing to fail." – Benjamin Franklin

My first experience with canoes was at a Boy Scout camp where I practiced entering a canoe without it tipping over and became experienced in emptying a capsized canoe full of water in the middle of a lake. I also learned a variety of strokes, including the forward stroke, draw stroke, back stroke, "J" stroke, "C" stroke, pry, variations of these strokes, and more.

At age four I lost my father to an industrial accident. My mother never remarried and raised my two sisters and me as best she could. Sending me to camps in the summer was one of many efforts she made to provide me with male role models and to see that I had some of the experiences I would have had if my father were alive. At the conclusion of the Boy Scout camp, I was presented with several merit badges. The one I was most proud of was for canoeing.

We did not own a canoe, but a family friend had two Willits Brothers canoes. These canoes were handcrafted by two brothers at their shop on Day Island in Tacoma, Washington. Each canoe was constructed of cedar planks attached by more than 7,000 copper tacks spaced every 1.5 in (3.8 cm). The exterior of the older of the two canoes had been covered with fiberglass. That was the canoe I was allowed to use, which I did quite often on Puget Sound. When I was in high school, I was allowed to use the newer canoe. This canoe was rarely used, and there wasn't a scratch or imperfection anywhere on its surface. My friend knew I could be trusted to keep it from touching the gravel beach and that I would wash off the salt water after every use. It was an honor to use this beautiful work of art.

After I graduated from high school, I was rarely back in the Olympia area where I grew up, so I had few opportunities to paddle the Willits canoes. Shortly after college I married Sue, then taught school in Tacoma for a year and a half and in Alaska for two years, managed a farm at a treatment center for emotionally disturbed boys on Cypress Island in the San Juan Island chain, and eventually settled on rural property between Gig Harbor and Port Orchard, WA. Teaching school and later becoming an elementary school principal along with helping raise our three children consumed nearly all of my time. When I was ready to retire, I had set foot in a canoe less than a dozen times over the previous thirty years.

A few years before I retired as a principal, Sue and I took a trip to Alaska to visit our daughter, which included a drive up the Steese Highway from Fairbanks to Circle City. In Circle City I met a couple who had just paddled the Yukon River from Dawson City in the Yukon. Listening to them share their story renewed my interest in canoeing, and I decided to make a similar paddle on the Yukon when I retired.

At that time I was only a few years from retirement, so when I returned home, I began my research. My eldest son, John, had met a lovely young woman, Dana Bauer, whom he later married. When I first met Dana's father, Phil, at his home near Vaughn, WA, I shared my dream of paddling the Yukon, and he asked if he could join the expedition but said he would like to paddle his kayak solo. I wanted to travel by canoe, so I needed to find a canoe partner.

Dan Linnell had been a close friend since the early 1970s. We both worked at the residential treatment center on Cypress Island and then left to teach in public schools at the same time. Dan and his family moved to Buckley, WA, where he taught math and coached at White River High School. My family and I settled on our two and a half acres, and I began teaching in Port Orchard. Dan and his family later moved to the Skagit Valley, where he taught at Sedro-Woolley High School until his retirement. Dan's family and mine stayed close for many years, celebrating New Year's Eves together, hiking in the Cascade Mountain Range, and camping. I knew Dan would be the perfect canoe partner, even though neither of us had much experience on rivers.

My other son, Reed, was married to a lovely girl who had grown up in Valdez, AK. Her father, Gary Mowry, indicated an interest in this expedition, but he wanted to paddle a canoe solo. Our team was set, and we began preparing for the expedition.

PERSEVERANCE

I purchased a book recommended by a friend, Derick Zimmer, written by Cliff Jacobson, who is known as one of the foremost experts on canoeing. The book, *Expedition Canoeing*, became the textbook we studied to prepare. This is a must read for anyone considering a paddle but especially for anyone planning an extended paddle that requires a variety of water conditions and spending nights camped along a river.

After several practice runs on rivers and lakes, honing our skills and developing the confidence we needed, we were ready for our Yukon expedition in June 2001. One week after school ended for the students, and one day after I had fulfilled my principal contract, we left for the Yukon River. Our expedition began in Whitehorse and ended three weeks later in Circle City, AK, some 700 mi (1,126 km) down the river. Unfortunately, Gary had severe back pain and was forced to pull out at Carmacks after just 189 mi (304 km) of paddling.

As we were completing our last stretch on the Yukon in the slow water of the Yukon Flats, we slowed to a leisurely pace and reflected on our three-week paddle. We agreed it would not be our last river trip.

I'm not sure how the Mackenzie River entered our thoughts, but it looked like a great challenge, and Phil and Dan agreed we should do some serious research. At that time few books had been written about paddling the Mackenzie. However, I found a book by Elizabeth Noel from Yellowknife, the capital of the Northwest Territories. In 1998, Elizabeth, her husband and son, and one of her son's friends paddled from Yellowknife, along the shore of Great Slave Lake, down the Mackenzie River, and out to the Arctic Ocean, finishing at the village of Tuktoyaktuk. Her book, *Reflections on a River*, chronicled their adventure. It also included a wealth of information, including packing lists, food planning tips, resources, recipes, and much more. As I developed a mile guide (which you can find at the end of this book), I included locations where the Noels found suitable camping spots. As it turned out, many of their sites were unsuitable on our expedition because of high water and erosion.

In the years between the Yukon trip and our Mackenzie expedition, we paddled several rivers, including a stretch of the Missouri River in Montana. Dan and I were committed to paddling my expedition canoe on the Mackenzie because of its size and stability as well as our success with it on the Yukon. Phil enjoyed paddling his kayak but was troubled by its limited space for gear and supplies. He was considering an expedition canoe similar to mine, but he needed to find someone to paddle with him.

Jacobson's book stresses the importance of choosing the right crew for an extended journey. All other factors take a back seat to compatibility. Phil knew he needed to pick someone who would be compatible with Dan and me as well as him. He decided that Don Hornbeck, a neighbor and retired dentist from Gig Harbor, WA, would meet this requirement. Don was not an experienced canoeist, but he had extensive experience backpacking in the forests and mountains of the Pacific Northwest. Don recalls Phil saying, "Hornbeck, how about you joining our little group, and we'll just canoe down the Mackenzie River to Tuktoyaktuk on the Arctic Ocean?"

"What a goofy idea," Don replied. However, needless to say, Don responded in the affirmative. In addition to his physical ability, he brought to our group a sense of humor that would be needed during stressful times.

On one of my trips to REI in Tacoma, I spotted a Mad River Revelation canoe hanging from the ceiling. I noted several scratches on the bottom and asked a salesman if they would be willing to reduce the price. We agreed on a price considerably below retail, and I immediately contacted Phil, who called Don. They hurried in to REI and walked away with the canoe that would carry them down the Mackenzie.

Phil and Don took their canoe out on Puget Sound and practiced paddling together. Phil practiced the strokes he would need to use in his position in the stern seat. Don needed to learn that from his position in the bow, his main job was providing power, and he needed to allow Phil to steer. The forward paddler has an unobstructed view of the river where he or she can see obstacles ahead. Both paddlers must communicate what they see and together determine the safest route forward.

Through our research we learned about the winds that could come up suddenly on the Mackenzie, creating rolling waves that could pour over the gunwales and potentially swamp the canoe. Don had experience making nylon stuff bags and other items for backpacking, and he volunteered to create spray skirts to cover our canoes and gear. His design was a huge success. The nylon spray skirts covered the entire canoe, including the gear and our bodies from the chest down, but would allow for an easy exit if we capsized.

I was responsible for the majority of the research into our expedition, including the Mackenzie River itself and its tributaries, islands, points of land, potential campsites, history, villages, populations, telephone access, and more. I gathered this information from a variety of resources to assist in our planning, to provide points of interest, and to understand some of the cultural elements of the people in locations we would be visiting on the journey. I put this together in what I call our "Mackenzie River Mile Guide." I've included the mile guide as an appendix at the end of this book. Please note that this is a resource created for our 2006 expedition, and some of the information is out of date, but it will at least provide a solid foundation for anyone considering such a journey.

As we neared the date of departure, Don's daughter, Molly, arranged for the four of us and our families to meet for dinner at a local restaurant. She was worried about her father taking on this potentially dangerous experience, paddling a canoe with no experience on a river and with a canoe partner she barely knew and with two others she didn't know at all. Displaying a sense of humor similar to her father's, she told us, "I just want to meet everyone before the wake."

Writing this book about our adventure took me over twelve years. During most of those years I was busy doing educational consulting and leadership coaching. I was also volunteering for a nonprofit organization based in British Columbia that did charity work in Ethiopia. I was able to make three visits to Ethiopia during that period. In my free time, I was building a 2,000-square-foot cabin (off grid and accessible only by boat) along the ocean on Hardy Island, approximately 60 mi (96.5 km) north of Vancouver, British Columbia. Once the cabin was finished, and I decided to retire for the last time, I began to focus on writing this book with conviction. Just over one year later, the manuscript was complete.

Although I have written several professional articles in journals and other publications, this is my first book.

John R. Richardson
Perseverance2006@gmail.com

Acknowledgments

Thank you to my wife, Sue, who encouraged me to take on this expedition, took care of so many things while I was gone, showed exceptional patience while I was writing at our cabin in British Columbia, and then read three different drafts, editing and making suggestions.

Thank you to my three friends who joined me on this journey. Dan Linnell has been my close friend since 1971 and my canoeing partner since 2001. I have always been able to count on his knowledge and skill to work with me in difficult conditions during our many voyages. Phil Bauer and Don Hornbeck were the perfect companions for Dan and me on this long and tedious journey. My friendship with these three before, during, and after the expedition is something I will always cherish. They have each spent many hours reading and providing input to this book. Thanks also to their families, who contributed in so many ways to the trip's success.

Thank you also to Elizabeth Noel, who kayaked from her hometown of Yellowknife, NWT, to Tuktoyaktuk in the summer of 1998. She published a book in 2000, *Reflections on a River*, based on a journal she kept of the expedition that she took with her husband, her son, and her son's friend. Her book was very useful as we planned our expedition, and you will see references to that trip throughout this book. Not only did she document their experiences, she also included tips on gear, food-planning ideas, checklists and menus, resources, and even recipes. Rivers are constantly changing from week to week and year to year, so her experiences varied significantly from ours. However, if you are planning to paddle the Mackenzie River, or if you just want another perspective on this route, I encourage you to read her book.

PERSEVERANCE

When asked about the most memorable part of the expedition, I answer without hesitation that it was the people we met along the way. Thanks to the following people who each contributed to the success of our trip: Dennis Estabrook in Manning, Alberta; Jo-Ann Jensen and Jack Kruger in Hay River; Angus Sanchez and George Bell in Jean Marie River; Robert Hardesty, Rita Betseda, and Victor Pauncha-Boot at the Willowlake River; Lloyd at Wrigley; Georgie McKay (NTCL), Lisa McDonald, Vera, Lorne, Gerry, Howard, Storm, and all the rest at the Canada Day Eve party in Norman Wells (and thank you for *The Sahtu Atlas*); Keith Hickling (Fish and Wildlife officer for the Sahtu region); Mike Jordan (RCMP) at Tulita; Wilfred McDonald at Oscar Creek; the staff at the band office in Tsiigehtchic; George Doolittle (RCMP), Sandy Hanson, Jennifer, and Eric in Inuvik; and all the others whose names I can't recall but will remember because of the kindness they showed.

All the photos I took on the expedition were in slide format. I narrowed the number down to approximately sixty and had them digitized. Thank you to Frank Arnoth at Digital Conversions LLC for the excellent conversion of my slides into digital format. Thank you also to Don Hornbeck for providing additional photos for the book.

Thank you to my good friend Lance Skidmore, who used his formative photographic skills to edit each photo and convert them to a high-quality black-and-white format. Thank you to Lance, Emery Hill, and Mike Snowden for reading one of my later drafts and providing input and suggestions.

ONE
On the Way

"A journey is best measured in friends rather than miles." – Tim Cahill (Author)

At 3:00 a.m. on the morning of June 13, 2006, my clock radio sprang to life, but my body didn't feel alive, and it certainly didn't spring. I rolled out of bed as quietly as possible, trying not to wake my wife, Sue. I showered, dressed, and then took the last items out of the garage, looking for a cranny somewhere in the bed of my F-250. Phil and Don had brought their canoe and most of their gear the night before, and between their gear and mine, the truck bed was almost full. The canoes were already secured to the Thule rack on top of the canopy over the truck bed. I had purchased the rack several years earlier, and it was not wide enough for two canoes, so Phil had a friend extend the width of the rails to accommodate the two Mad River Revelations. With the canoes strapped down, they extended out beyond the sides of the truck but no farther than the side mirrors, so we were satisfied.

Just before 4:00 a.m., Phil and Don arrived and loaded the remainder of their gear into the truck. We peered under the canopy, looking at our load of dry bags, paddles, life jackets, food, clothing, boots, and more, hoping Dan had packed light. In less than half an hour, I said goodbye to Sue, and we headed north.

After a stop for diesel just north of Tacoma, I set the cruise control at 60 mph and didn't take it off until we arrived in Mount Vernon, where we picked up Dan. Somehow we managed to wedge Dan's gear into the truck, and then we drove to Bellingham. We stopped at my son Reed's home to see three of my grandchildren: Nathaniel, Reed Evan, and our newest granddaughter, Caitlyn.

PERSEVERANCE

Caitlyn had been born just three weeks prior, one month premature. Within two hours after her birth, Caitlyn turned blue and was loaded into a helicopter and medevaced to Seattle's Children's Hospital. She spent two and a half weeks in intensive care before she was out of danger. She had just been released from the hospital, and I was elated at how much she had grown and how healthy she looked.

We arrived at the Canadian border crossing at Sumas, WA, at 9:30 a.m. A customs officer asked us for our proof of citizenship. I handed her my passport, and Phil, Don, and Dan passed on their driver's licenses. The grim look on her face told me things weren't going to go well.

"A driver's license is not a proof of citizenship," she said. "Anyone can get a driver's license." She explained that we would need to go inside, but first she asked if we had any alcohol, tobacco, or firearms. Phil told her of the cigars he had packed in the back, and we explained that we were carrying two rifles. She said we would need to register them inside.

We parked the truck outside the customs office and walked in through the double doors. We were excited to be on our way and entered with smiles on our faces and a bit of laughter. I don't know if a grim affect is part of the training for customs officers, but they were having no part of the frivolity these four Americans were displaying.

Don found his passport in the back of the truck, but Phil and Dan were forced to listen to another lecture about proof of citizenship. The officer took their driver's licenses and additional information to a room that was out of sight from the counter. We sat for nearly thirty minutes until she returned with permission to enter the country. But that permission was not granted until she gave yet another lecture about proof of citizenship. Then we were directed to another counter to register our rifles.

When we crossed the border five years earlier en route to the Yukon River, we registered three rifles. A new Canadian law had just come into effect, requiring a $25 fee for each person carrying up to three firearms. We considered saying that all the rifles belonged to one person to save $50 but thought better of it. When we explained that the rifles belonged to Phil, Dan, and Gary, the officer asked, "Are you sure they don't all belong to one person? Because if they did, you'd only have to pay twenty-five dollars." We appreciated the suggestion and told her that they all belonged to Dan. "I thought so," she replied and charged us only $25.

Now, five years later, we decided to claim that both of our rifles belonged to Dan. However, that just led to another lecture. "You can only bring one rifle per person," the officer said. Apparently, the law had changed. I suggested to Dan that he give one of his rifles to Phil, but my suggestion was not appreciated. "You can't do that!" the officer shouted.

When Dan admitted that one of the rifles belonged to Phil, the officer responded in a very official tone. "So, you told me an untruth." I had visions of one or all of us spending a night in a Canadian jail. In a repentant tone, Dan admitted he had indeed told an untruth. I explained our experience five years earlier at that same border crossing, where a border officer suggested we register all three rifles with one person to save on fees. I received a strong, angry look and an even angrier response. "No one would do that!" he said. I thought about arguing my point, but he was holding all the cards, so I kept my mouth shut and watched him march away, leaving us standing at the counter for several minutes. Eventually, he returned with two forms. Dan and Phil completed the forms, each paying $25, and we were allowed to continue on our way. We walked out of the office with serious looks on our faces and made no comments until we reached Highway 1. At that point, we all started laughing and reminding Dan that he had told an "untruth."

Highway 1 took us through Abbotsford, and we arrived almost an hour later than planned in Hope, British Columbia. Hope is a lovely little town nestled along the Fraser River with a population of a little more than 6,000. We found the nearest liquor store and purchased a couple of bottles of Yukon Jack, advertised as "The Black Sheep of Canadian Liquors." None of us are heavy drinkers, but we wanted to continue the tradition we began on the Yukon River of having a shot of Yukon Jack every evening to celebrate each day's accomplishments. On days when we felt our accomplishments were extraordinary, we would celebrate twice.

From Hope we continued on Highway 1 through the Fraser Canyon to the small community of Cache Creek, where we filled our tank with diesel. Highway 1 turns east there, but we continued north on Highway 97 to Quesnel. Seven and a half mi (12 km) north of Quesnel is Ten Mile Lake Provincial Park, where we set up camp for the night. We had been up since 3:00 a.m. and traveled more than 530 mi (853 km) and were ready to eat and get to bed. Dan brought venison steaks and beer dogs, which we enjoyed immensely. By 9:30 p.m. we were in our tents enjoying the last light of the warm summer evening.

PERSEVERANCE

Sometime during the night, I was awakened by the light spatter of raindrops on my tent. I hadn't expected rain, so I hadn't put on my fly. I had a small tarp inside the tent, so I climbed out and stretched it across the tent. Soon the light rain turned to a heavy downpour, and water began seeping into the tent where the tarp didn't cover. By 6:00 a.m., the bottom of my sleeping bag was soaked, and I lay there trying to decide what to do. I was ready to get up, but my raincoat was somewhere in the back of the truck.

At 6:30 a.m. I crawled out and began the daily ritual of stuffing my sleeping bag into its stuff bag and breaking down my tent. The rain had receded, but light drops were still coming down. We were all up by then, and we began packing our gear into the truck. We had been very careful with our packing until then, but that morning we skipped breakfast and stuffed our wet gear into the back of the truck, so we could be on our way.

As we drove, the rain subsided, and when we reached Prince George, the pavement was dry. We ate breakfast at Denny's before continuing north toward Dawson Creek. It has a population of more than 11,000 and is the starting point for the Alaska Highway. Following lunch at Tim Hortons, we struck out east, crossing into Alberta. We followed Highway 49 to the junction with Highway 2 and then to Highway 35, also known as the Mackenzie Route.

We stopped for diesel in Manning, Alberta. While we were waiting to fill up, a man in a Chevrolet pickup made a U-turn in the street in front of us and drove into the service station. He introduced himself as Dennis Estabrook. He had seen our canoes and was interested in our destination. When we told him our plans, he said he would see us the next day at the campground in Fort Providence, where he and some friends would be fishing.

Forty miles (65 km) north of Manning, at the Twin Lakes Provincial Recreation Area campground, we made camp for the night. We unloaded our wet gear and laid it out to dry. A warm wind combined with the arctic sun dried things quickly. The sky to the east was becoming dark, but we were better prepared than the previous night, and the covered picnic area was destined to help keep us dry.

Lightning began in the distance and was soon surrounding us with frequent bursts of light. A short shower doused our tents, but then the sky became lighter. We prepared dinner in the picnic area, protected from the moisture. By the time we climbed into our tents at 9:00 p.m., they were nearly dry.

By morning a heavy dew blanketed everything that wasn't covered. After a breakfast of oatmeal and breakfast bars, we loaded up and were on the road by 7:45 a.m. At High Level we filled up with diesel and continued on, stopping at the visitor center on the border of the Northwest Territories where Highway 35 becomes NWT Highway 1. There we were able to purchase fishing licenses and acquire road and ferry information.

Our next stop was at Alexandra Falls, a massive 109-foot (33-m) fall of water from Hay River. The water was brown with silt, and at the base of the falls, bubbles formed into a brown froth that continued down the river for miles.

One of many decisions that must be made for any expedition is what to do about transportation. We could have left the truck at Fort Providence, our launch point. However, returning to Great Slave Lake with four people, two canoes, and all our gear would be difficult and expensive. One option we considered was to drive to our launch point, unload our canoes and gear, and then I would drive to Inuvik, the only town in the Mackenzie Delta accessible by road. Then I could fly back to Fort Providence, where we could begin the trip, and the truck would be waiting for us at Inuvik. The downside of this was that Dan, Phil, and Don would need to wait for my return, four days or longer depending on what kind of flight arrangements I could make. In addition, the diesel for the drive to Inuvik as well as the cost of the return flight could be expensive.

Don took it upon himself to research transportation options and came up with an excellent solution. He found that all the villages along the Mackenzie River received their supplies by barge. The only company providing this service was the Northern Transportation Company Limited (NTCL). This would save us several days of waiting, and the cost would be less than the additional driving and the flight. I emailed NCTL and arranged to have the truck barged from Hay River to Inuvik. The representative I worked with was Jo-Ann Jensen, who was extremely helpful and patient with me as I asked a variety of questions about the process.

At Enterprise we turned onto NWT Highway 2 and drove approximately 25 mi (40 km) to Hay River. We stopped at the NTCL shipyards and made final arrangements for barging the truck to Inuvik and for shipping two containers of additional supplies to the halfway point of our expedition, Norman Wells.

We learned that the barge to Norman Wells was scheduled to leave the following day, so we needed our containers ready for shipping immediately. We dug into our gear and separated our supplies into two categories: those needed

PERSEVERANCE

for the first half of the trip and those needed on the second half. Our stove fuel was in two cans, so that decision was easy. Other decisions were not. Better advance planning for the separation of our supplies for the halfway point was something to remember for another expedition. Nevertheless, in less than an hour, our supplies were separated, and the items to be shipped were placed into a cardboard box and a plastic tub, strapped tight with duct tape. Jo-Ann took our boxes and charged us the minimum amount, $65 for up to 600 lbs.

Our next stop was the Greyhound bus station, where we arranged for Phil and me to be transported to Fort Providence the next day, after we left my truck at NTCL.

Before leaving Hay River, we stopped at a local market and purchased potatoes, carrots, cabbage, apples, lettuce, and salad dressing. We found a liquor store, purchased a case of beer, and followed Highway 2 back to Highway 1, where we turned north toward Fort Providence.

Our first glimpse of the Mackenzie River was at the Mackenzie River ferry crossing, two and a half hours after leaving Hay River. This small free ferry, the *Merv Hardie*, crossed the river near the outflow point of Great Slave Lake. The ferry landing consisted primarily of gravel. Heavy equipment was standing by to make repairs where the swift river was constantly washing the gravel away. When the water level subsided, gravel stored in tall piles was used to extend the landing as the edge of the river crept outward. In winter, such constant repairs were not necessary because as the river froze and stabilized, vehicles were able to cross on thick ice.

The ferry was just leaving from the other side as we arrived. Within twenty minutes we were on the ferry and crossing the Mackenzie. The river was a light-brown color, full of silt from the spring runoff of the many rivers and streams flowing into it. The wind was blowing, but there were no whitecaps, and it looked good for canoeing. We noticed the river was extremely high, and we discussed the challenge of finding a suitable place to launch our canoes.

In 2008, construction began on a bridge that eventually replaced the Merv Hardie *ferry. The project wasn't completed until more than four years later. On November 30, 2012, the Deh Cho Bridge was opened to traffic. This is the only bridge crossing the Mackenzie River.*

Our ten-minute crossing was smooth and uneventful. The landing site was approximately 5 mi (8 km) from the Fort Providence Territorial Park

Campground, where we would be spending the next two nights. Three and a half mi (5.6 km) from the ferry, we turned onto the road that would take us to the campground and the village. If we hadn't turned, we would have eventually reached the city of Yellowknife, the capital of the Northwest Territories.

The campground was nearly full, and the only campsites remaining had deep puddles of rainwater and mud. In addition, large piles of manure were everywhere, left behind by the large herds of wood bison living in the area. We chose the best of what was left and began setting up camp. Dennis Estabrook, the person we met in Manning, walked across the road as we were setting up. He and his friends were camped across from our site. He showed us a good-sized northern pike that he had caught that afternoon.

The campground was a haven for mosquitoes. Between the mud, standing water, and manure, they had found a happy home. That made for a miserable time as we set up camp, swatting mosquitos with one hand while carrying our gear with the other. Quickly, we set up our 15-x-15-ft (4.5-x4.5-m) Tundra tent. The nylon top and sides made of netting had provided us with many enjoyable evenings away from pesky insects on our previous trips. It was a gift from my wife when I retired and left on my Yukon River expedition in 2001.

We put most of our gear in the Tundra tent and then began setting up our personal tents. We had captured hundreds of mosquitos in the Tundra tent, but thankfully, the others couldn't get in. Within a few minutes, we killed most of them between our clapping hands as they danced on the netting.

The river was close by, but a steep bank and high water would prevent us from launching at the campground. Dan and I drove into Fort Providence to look for a suitable launch site.

Fort Providence is a small village of approximately 750 inhabitants, mostly Aboriginal. It lies on a patch of land surrounded by swamp, muskeg, and the Mackenzie River. At the far end of town, approximately 2.5 mi (4 km) from the campground, was the public boat launch. We spoke to two men there and learned it was the only suitable location to begin our trip. The challenge would be to find a way to transport our canoes and gear to the launch site the next day, since by then our truck would be at the NCTL shipyard.

In Fort Providence, we saw several wood bison walking thorough yards and down the gravel streets. Near the campground, we saw two bulls eating grass at the edge of the airport.

PERSEVERANCE

The bison in Fort Providence outnumber the human inhabitants by nearly three to one. The area was designated the Mackenzie Bison Sanctuary in the early 1960s to protect these enormous animals. One hundred years ago, nearly 200,000 bison roamed the area. Today, the bison population is around 2,000. They seem to understand that it is a protected area as cars and people don't seem to bother them.

Back at camp we rubbed generous amounts of insect repellent on our exposed arms and faces and then prepared dinner under the Tundra tent—a feast of venison steak, beer dogs, beans, and salad. Throughout dinner we were attacked by mosquitos, which hit our skin and bounced off because they didn't like landing on the repellent. The more we killed the mosquitos, the more they came, apparently coming up out of the ground.

After dinner, Don, Dan, and I drove to a store/bar/restaurant out on the main highway to call home. It would be the last time we would be in contact with our families for several days. Sue was home when I called and it was good to hear her voice. It was also a bit sad because she said she was feeling "empty" with me being gone for so long.

We returned to camp, and I climbed into my tent at about 10:30 p.m., the sun still bright in the western sky. As I lay there, I thought about the next day when Phil and I would be taking the truck back to Hay River for its trip down the Mackenzie.

TWO
The Day Before the Beginning

"If we walk in the woods, we must feed mosquitoes." – Ralph Waldo Emerson

Friday, June 16, 2006 – Fort Providence

I slept well and woke up at 7:00 a.m. to a warm, sunny day. My success killing all the mosquitoes before I went to sleep made for a pleasant night. I fell asleep to the hum of thousands of the little parasites trying every possible way to enter the tent. Hundreds were under the fly and in the vestibule, tapping on the netting. I had left my bottle of Jungle Juice insect repellent out where it would be handy in the Tundra tent because I knew I would be fighting the little critters there. I got dressed, scuttled outside, and raced for the Tundra tent. I'm sure at least a hundred mosquitoes were able to get inside as I passed through the doorway. However, I covered my exposed skin with repellent and was able to relax

Dan, Phil, and Don were up soon after me, and for the next half hour, in a united effort, we killed mosquitoes between our clapping hands. As hard as we worked, we didn't seem to reduce their numbers. We finally gave up and lathered ourselves with more Jungle Juice. Breakfast consisted of instant oatmeal and breakfast bars, the same breakfast we would eat every day for the next month.

After breakfast it was time to begin preparing for the trip back to Hay River. We took the canoes down from the rack on top of the truck. All our gear needed to be sorted and stored under tarps because this would be the last day we would see the truck until we reached Inuvik. We considered loading the canoes at the campsite to make sure everything would fit but chose to take the chance of overpacking, so we wouldn't have to contend with the mosquitos, which were so thick that I would occasionally suck them into my nostrils or into my mouth. The Jungle Juice kept them from landing, but the more determined ones continued to pelt my face and hands before bouncing away from the liquid deterrent. I was so irritated that I finally pulled out my mosquito head net.

At 9:30 a.m., Phil and I climbed into the truck and began our two-hour drive back to Hay River. The air conditioning provided a comfortable change from the heat of the day.

Our first stop in Hay River was the RCMP office. We filled out a trip report to let them know we would be on the river. In addition to filling out three pages of forms and attaching our itinerary, names of next of kin, and their phone numbers, we also gave them the number of our satellite phone. The friendly woman who helped us with the report recommended that we stop by the Coast Guard station and meet Jack Kruger. "Jack appreciates meeting river travelers before they depart," she said.

Before we met with Jack, we stopped by Field's Variety Store to purchase mosquito coils, bath towels, and dish towels. They had everything except the mosquito coils. At a friend's home in British Columbia, I had seen a mosquito zapper shaped like a small tennis racket and asked Phil if he was aware of them. He scoffed as I asked the clerk if they had any for sale. She explained that they usually had them, but they were out of stock, so I headed for the local Ace Hardware, which I'd seen on our way into town. Phil told me it was a waste of time, but I persisted, and we were able to find them. I bought one for me and, despite Phil's resistance, purchased one for the group to have in the Tundra tent. Ace also had mosquito coils, so we purchased two boxes and were now ready to do battle with the nemesis that drove humans and animals alike into fits of rage. After lunch at a bakery across the street, we filled the truck with diesel and then set out for the Coast Guard station to meet Jack Kruger.

Jack was a friendly fellow who had answers to all our questions. Phil asked if the mosquitos were as bad along the river as they were at Fort Providence. "No," Jack replied emphatically. "Fort Providence is the worst spot for mosquitos on the river." When Phil asked about locations to pull out and make camp, Jack showed us digital photos of the river on his computer. "The RCMP are stationed at every village along the river," he informed us. Although he was very friendly and responded to all our inquiries, I had a feeling he was concerned that we were taking on something for which we might not be adequately prepared. When I gave him a copy of the mile guide I had prepared for the trip, his hesitancy disappeared. "With the planning shown here, you guys know what you're doing," he said. Then he wished us well as we left the office.

In one of the pictures Jack had shown us was a small cruise ship, the *Noweta*. It was 103 ft (31.4 m) long and was built in 1971. As we drove down to a campground along Great Slave Lake, we saw the *Noweta* tied to a pier and being readied for a party onboard. Soon, the first of several excursions up and down the river between Fort Providence and Inuvik would begin. Each trip took eight days downriver and ten days against the current back to Fort Providence. We expected to see the ship on our expedition to Inuvik.

Great Slave Lake is a massive body of water, 291 mi (468 km) long and 126 mi (203 km) wide. It's the tenth-largest lake in the world and the deepest lake in North America, 2,014 ft (614 m) at its deepest spot.

The wind was blowing as we reached the lake and walked along the gravel beach. Large waves crashed on the shore, making it seem like we were on the coast of the Pacific Ocean.

It was soon time to drive to the NTCL shipyard to leave the truck. I drove it onto the scales to determine the weight and the cost of transportation to Inuvik. We met Jo-Ann in the office and paid her $1,782.88 (approximately US$1,600). In return, she gave each of us an NTCL cap.

A college student working during the summer for NTCL gave us a ride to the Greyhound bus station. We waited for an hour until our bus driver, Jerry, ushered us, his only passengers, aboard. Jerry was very friendly and explained this was just his third trip as a bus driver, having begun the job only a few days before. He had been laid off as a truck driver transporting fuel to the diamond mine north of Yellowknife. He described the elaborate security system for transportation between Yellowknife and the mine. "Each truck must be exactly five kilometers from other trucks and must travel no faster than twenty-five kilometers per hour. All trucks are monitored closely and are told to speed up or slow down to keep the five-kilometer distance between them." When winter came, and the roads firmed up, Jerry expected to be called back.

We picked up two passengers in the small community of Enterprise. Our two-hour bus ride came to an end as we arrived at Fort Providence. Jerry dropped us off at the entrance to the provincial park, and we walked to our campsite. Phil and I unzipped the Tundra tent's mosquito netting and entered along with hundreds of mosquitos. Dan and Don had been killing mosquitos all day and weren't happy that we had brought more inside. I reached into the bag I was carrying and pulled out a zapper. They were both curious, and Phil was skeptical. As the racket-like instrument hit each mosquito, a spark, accompanied by a zapping sound, incinerated the pests. "Give me that!" Phil said, and he started killing the skeeters by the dozens. From that point on, Phil was a believer.

With most of the mosquitos electrocuted, we had a pleasant dinner, and Phil and I shared our experiences in Hay River. When we showed them our hats, we realized we should have asked for two more, one each for Dan and Don.

We began speculating on the best way to get our canoes loaded and onto the river. The riverbank was steep and at least 30 ft (9 m) high. The river was still rushing by at a feverish clip. We didn't look forward to carrying our canoes and gear 2.5 mi (4 km) to the boat launch, which would take at least three trips. Dennis Estabrook came over from his camp spot and offered to take us and our gear to the boat launch in his truck. Problem solved!

With our plans firmly in place for the next day, we settled down for the night. Shortly after I had exterminated the invading insects and crawled into my sleeping bag, the rain began. I had put up my fly, so I would be staying dry. It soon turned into a gully washer, and I heard Dan shout a four-letter expletive. He had decided to sleep in the Tundra tent but the heavy rain caused the roof to sag and collect a large pool of water. The tent was about to collapse, so Dan used a canoe paddle to push up on the ceiling. It was an effective maneuver to get the water off the tent, but the weight caused the tent to lean in such a way that when the water ran off, most of it washed inside, soaking Dan and much of his gear.

Once the rain subsided, I determined that Dan had everything under control, so I crawled back into my sleeping bag and fell asleep.

THREE
Departure

"Twenty years from now you will be more disappointed by the things you didn't do than by the ones you did do. So throw off the bowlines. Sail away from the safe harbor. Catch the trade winds in your sails. Explore. Dream. Discover." – Mark Twain

Saturday, June 17, 2007 – Fort Providence

We were out of our tents and into the Tundra tent by 8:00 a.m., eating oatmeal and breakfast bars. Once we were packed and ready, Dennis drove over to our campsite and gave us the keys to his truck.

We loaded Don and Phil's canoe and gear into the truck bed, and Phil and Don drove the truck to the boat launch before returning for Dan and me and all our gear. We loaded up and drove through the town, past the little white houses and the church with its steeple standing high above all the other buildings. Bison roamed through the streets and cropped grass in the yards, fertilizing as they went.

The Fort Providence boat launch was situated in a small backwater, protected from the current by a small point of land. The launch consisted of a slab of cement, partially covered by gravel that had worked its way over from the beaches on either side. The river was heavy with silt, and we were able to see only a couple of inches down.

Once we were unloaded, Phil drove the truck back to pick up Dennis. A couple of Aboriginal men wandered up and sat down to watch the spectacle, appearing unconvinced that we knew what we were doing.

PERSEVERANCE

A great deal of planning went into choosing our gear, making sure each item was needed, and that all the items would fit into the canoe. Both canoes were Mad River Revelations, expedition canoes made from a durable product called Royalex, a composite material with an outer layer of vinyl and hard acrylonitrile butadiene styrene plastic (ABS) and an inner layer of ABS foam, bonded together using heat.

I first learned of this material two decades ago in talking with a person I met at a gas station in Alaska. I was admiring his Old Town Tripper on the top of his truck. I hadn't yet purchased a canoe, and I asked him if he was happy with his Tripper. He took me over to his truck and showed me a small wrinkle that ran from gunwale to gunwale in the center of the canoe. He shared an experience where he capsized in a fast-moving river. The bottom of the canoe was facing downstream and the open portion was facing upstream. As the canoe drifted, the bottom caught on a large rock, and the power of the river bent the canoe in half. When he was able to free the canoe, he pulled it ashore and was able to push it back to its original shape. "Whatever canoe you buy," he said, "make sure it's made of Royalex." Thus, my research prior to purchasing a canoe had one main element: it had to be made of Royalex. A friend, Derick Zimmer, who had paddled the entire length of the Yukon River swore by his Mad River Revelation, so that's what I settled on.

The first trip planned for the canoe was the Yukon River in 2001, the day after I retired from eleven years of teaching and twenty-three years as an elementary school principal. I spent all of those twenty-three years as principal of Sunnyslope Elementary School in Port Orchard, WA. My staff knew I was about to buy the canoe, and they surprised me by giving it to me as a retirement gift. Every day I paddle that canoe, I appreciate their friendship and generosity.

I installed tie-downs on the floor of the canoe with "D" rings for lashing down our gear. Everything was stowed in dry bags or in sealed plastic bags inside plastic tubs. Derick Zimmer had used trash compactor bags because of their size and durability. I am still using the same plastic bags I purchased in 2001. They have traveled over 2,500 mi (4,025 km) with me on numerous rivers and lakes in Alaska, British Columbia, the Northwest Territories, Washington, Idaho, and Montana.

All the dry bags and tubs were lashed down securely, so they would stay with the canoe if we should capsize. We also attached painter lines to the bow and stern.

Painter lines are ropes made of polypropylene. They are lightweight and float on the water's surface. Each line is 25 ft (7.6 m) long and bunched under a shock cord *attached in a loop to the top of the canoe deck. Painters are used for lining (pulling) the canoe along the edge of the river. Bunching the painter on the deck makes it easy to grab and pull the canoe to shore in case it capsizes. In addition to the painters, we also tied a 65-foot (20-m) polypropylene throw rope to the bow of the canoe and kept it inside within easy reach of the paddler in the bow.*

When Phil and Dennis arrived, we were ready to begin our expedition, which would take us more than 900 mi (1,449 km) down the Mackenzie River. At 10:35 a.m. we said farewell to Dennis and the locals who came to watch us depart. They wished us well as we climbed in and pushed off.

As we left the boat launch and rounded the small point, the current took us swiftly downriver. Several small boats were on the river, and several cabins lined the shore. As we paddled to the center of the river, I looked back at the pristine little village, its church steeple the most visible landmark.

Dan and I paddled faster than Phil and Don, and we slowly increased our distance from their canoe. We tried to keep them in sight for safety, but soon we found ourselves more than a mile apart. Several small islands were in that section of the river, and we were concerned that Phil and Don might take a different route, and we would lose sight of them entirely. It was 12:45 p.m., so Dan and I stopped at a small eroding island to stretch, have a bite to eat, and wait for them to catch up. The shoreline was muddy, and it was difficult to find a place to sit. It was also steep and slippery, which made it difficult to move up to dryer land. Once the canoe was tied securely to a small tree, we sat down to eat.

We expected Phil and Don would stop with us, but they had paddled to the left of a larger island, out of sight. When we realized what had happened, we pushed off and began looking for them. We were near Mills Lake, a large body of water formed by the widening of the Mackenzie River. It is circular in shape and approximately 12.5 mi (20 km) wide. It's a sanctuary for many birds and other wildlife, including mosquitoes, as we soon discovered. Ducks, eagles, kingfishers, and other birds kept us entertained as we paddled into the wide expanse of the river. Seagulls and terns flew above us, and a pair of mallards skittered across the water, moving away from the canoe's path. We passed four boats of fishermen along the shoreline but didn't see a fish being reeled in. As we passed a long island on our left, we were relieved to see Phil and Don paddling on the other side. Soon we came together and continued on.

PERSEVERANCE

The temperature was in the high 80s Fahrenheit (low 30s Celsius) with only an occasional breeze. I wanted to take off my shirt, but there were a few hitchhiking mosquitoes in the canoe, waiting for the chance to find open skin.

The lake was very high and spread into the vegetation along the shore. As the day wore on, we began looking for a suitable area to make camp. At 5:30 p.m. we found a small gravel area along the shore. The patch of gravel was so small that we determined it wasn't suitable for a camp, so we decided to have our dinner there and then move on to find a better location.

Dan, Phil, and I had been paddling together for five years, but this was Don's first trip with us. Our dinner of choice is foil dinners cooked on the coals of a wood fire. The ingredients changed from day to day, but they usually included diced potatoes, carrots, cabbage, and onion. All of these vegetables kept well in the bottom of our canoes for a long time. We always included sausage, pepperoni, or fish. If we come into a town with a grocery store, we purchased other meats for our dinners.

Phil began cutting up the potatoes, carrots, cabbage, and sausage while Dan, Don, and I scrounged for dry wood to build a fire. I was able to find dry grass and reeds, and Don found some small sticks. Dan found a large branch and sawed logs from it that would provide good coals for cooking. Using sheets of heavy aluminum foil, we divided up the vegetables and sausage, added spices, olive oil, and a few tablespoons of water, then folded the foil around the food, making sure it was tightly sealed. If the foil was not securely sealed, or if it was punctured, the liquids would escape, and the food would burn.

After the coals had died down sufficiently, we scattered them into a flat surface for our foil dinners. Twenty-five minutes later, the food was ready. We used flat sticks to lift the dinners from the fire and place them on our plates. The meal was exquisite.

After dinner we packed up and pushed off into the lake to begin our search for a suitable campsite. There was no breeze, and the lake was as smooth as a tabletop. Far from the vegetation along the shore, the mosquitoes didn't bother us. It was warm and peaceful as we dipped our paddles in a synchronized rhythm.

After about three hours of paddling, we spotted an area that we thought might be sufficient, so Dan and I paddled ashore while Phil and Don watched from a distance. Dan charged through the vegetation and up to a clear area we had spotted from the lake. Within minutes he came running back through the brush, waving his hands wildly about his head. "Let's get out of here!" he screamed. At first I thought he might have encountered a bear, but as he came closer, I saw that he was surrounded by thousands of mosquitoes. Unfortunately, he brought the pests into the canoe with him, so I put on an extra coat of Jungle Juice. He explained that the area was unsuitable for a camp, but even if it were, we weren't staying there. As we paddled out into the lake, we were able to escape most of the insects but a few seemed to like our company.

A 10:30 p.m. we spotted a small gravel beach about a foot above the water level. We landed and were able to smooth out the gravel to create level ground for our tents. Behind the beach was a swampy area, a breeding ground for mosquitoes. We pitched our tents quickly, had a shot of Yukon Jack, and then crawled in for the night. I was thankful I had found my mosquito zapper in Hay River and was able to clear my tent of insects. I looked over my map and estimated that we had traveled over 34 mi (54.7 km).

34.5 mi (54.7 km) traveled today

Campsite location along Mills Lake: N61°19'30" W118°26'37"

FOUR
Big Fish and High Water

"There is a moment during every fight with a strong fish when you wonder whether it or you will win the battle." – Fennel Hudson (Outdoorsman and Author)

Sunday, June 18, 2007 – Downriver from Mills Lake

The sun was shining brightly when we climbed out of our tents at 7:30 a.m. A heavy dew had soaked our tent flies, so we spread them out over bushes while we fixed breakfast and packed up our gear. By 10:00 a.m. we were on the water and enjoying the beautiful weather. It took a few minutes for my arms to begin working, but soon we were in rhythm, moving along rapidly. The water was very still on Mills Lake with no noticeable current. We were no longer in the widest portion of the lake, even though the distant shore was more than 2 mi (3.2 km) away.

At 11:20 a.m. we stopped at a gravel beach where cabins and outhouses were built on a bank away from the water. Drying racks indicated it was a fishing camp, used by the Aboriginals to prepare fish for the winter. We had snacks before moving on again.

When I began planning this trip, I searched for books written by others who had traveled the river. Most of the books I found were old and didn't provide me with the type of information I was looking for. One book, Reflections on a River *by Elizabeth Noel, was exactly what I had hoped to find. Elizabeth lives in Yellowknife, and she, her husband and son, and their son's friend kayaked from Yellowknife to Tuktoyaktuk on the Arctic Ocean. The book details their adventure, including GPS coordinates of each stop. In reading her book, I felt as if I were traveling with her family. As our own trip progressed, it felt like much of what I saw I had seen before. Her book was a blessing in planning our trip.*

Another important element in our planning was Google Earth. By tracing the entire path of the river and using the GPS coordinates Elizabeth provided, I was able to focus on their campsites and the other locations she had identified.

One such location was Noel's Campsite #13 along a creek at the following coordinates: N61°18'283" W118°43'398." Elizabeth described a suitable campsite with a teepee frame and a firepit. Her husband and son swam in unusually warm water and considered going up the creek to try to find the source of the warmth.

Dan and I were committed to stopping at the creek that Elizabeth mentioned and to paddle upstream to determine if a hot spring was the source of the warm water. We had crossed to the north side of the river, and just before 12:30 p.m., we reached the stream. It appeared to be more of a slough, at the same level as the swollen Mackenzie.

As we entered through the grass and small bushes at the entrance, we saw bubbling and thrashing on the surface. Our first reaction was surprise and then excitement as we realized that large northern pike were schooling in the slough. Dan had his fishing pole handy, and I steadied the canoe against the current while he cast his lure where there was movement in the water.

Just then, Phil and Don came paddling by. "Stop! Fish!" I yelled, but they were too far away to hear me. I suspect they saw us leave the river, thought we were stopping to relieve ourselves, and took the opportunity to take the lead for a while. The last I saw was both of them digging their paddles deep and hard to gain some distance before we were back on the water.

On his first cast, Dan caught a pike that was about 20 in (50 cm) long. A fair current was trying to push us back into the river, so I was busy keeping the canoe in the slough. My pole was on the floor of the canoe and not yet assembled, but I couldn't put it together at the same time I was fighting the current. After three more casts and three more fish of similar size, which Dan released, he handed his pole to me, and he paddled in the bow seat to keep us in the slough.

On my first cast, I hooked into a big fish. It stayed down, and I wasn't able to see it through the coffee-colored water. I fought it for several minutes until it surfaced near the bow of the canoe. Dan let out a whoop. "It's a big one!" he yelled. It went down again, but I was reluctant to tug too much on Dan's eight-pound test leader.

Dan paddled us to shore near the camping spot with the teepee frame and firepit, and I climbed out and continued my fight with the large pike. As it tired, I was able to drag it close to shore. Dan put his hands under it and threw it onto the beach. Its big, wide mouth opened and closed as it tried to bite anything it could find with its razor-sharp teeth. Dan picked up a pole he found near the firepit and hit it on the head until it stopped thrashing about.

At that moment, fish scales would have come in handy, but that wasn't something we had considered when we packed and probably wouldn't have included anyway. We could only guess the weight, but we were able to measure it at 39 in (100 cm). Although it seemed like a prize catch, northern pike are known to grow up to 59 in (150 cm) in length.

Dan fished a while longer and hooked one so deep in its throat that it would have surely died if we tried to pull out the lure, so we killed it and then cleaned both fish. The only room inside the canoe for the fish was around our feet, and we didn't want squashed pike for dinner, so we tied a rope through their gills and attached them to the stern. We climbed back in the canoe and were off again, dragging two northern pike behind us.

Our original purpose of entering the stream was soon forgotten due to our fishing experience of a lifetime. However, we didn't find the water to be any warmer than the river, so our dream of bathing in a hot spring wasn't likely to become a reality anyway.

Phil and Don had succeeded in putting a lot of distance between us, but after an hour of paddling, we saw them pulled alongside the river near a small stream. As we paddled toward them, Phil excitedly held up a pike he had just caught, which I estimated to be about 18 in (46 cm) long. Phil may dispute my estimate, but when I lifted my fish out of the water, he threw his back in.

The temperature was still in the 80s, and I was sweating profusely under my shirt and life jacket. We all decided to paddle to a point in the distance to fix dinner and then paddle farther to make our camp.

Dan and I were far ahead when we reached the point and found an uneven gravel beach that looked like a respectable site to cook dinner. We leveled out an area for our chairs, gathered firewood, and started a small fire. Phil and Don soon arrived. "Do you need any ice?" Don shouted, pointing to a mound of gravel with a light spot in the center just downriver from us.

When winter arrives in the Mackenzie River Valley, temperatures can drop to -60°F (-51°C) and lower. Ice forms several feet thick, and as the spring temperatures moderate, the ice begins to melt and eventually flows downstream, breaking up into massive chunks that crash against each other and tear away the riverbanks, bringing dirt, rock, trees, and other vegetation into the river. Some of this ice is pushed onto the shoreline, where it slowly melts in warmer weather. "Breakup," as it is called throughout the northern regions of Canada and the US, occurred long before we began our expedition. Don had made the first sighting of standing ice just a few hundred feet from our dinner stop.

I grabbed Dan's axe and my collapsible bucket and hiked down the beach. As I approached the mass of ice, I realized it was much larger than it had first appeared. I scraped away the gravel and dirt, exposing clean, clear ice, which I chopped into small chunks, so we could cool the one can of beer, one can of Coca Cola, and a Diet Pepsi that remained in our supplies.

When I returned, Phil and Dan were cutting up vegetables and preparing them for the foil dinner. Dan cut up some of the pike and put it in a separate foil wrapping with seasonings. When the fire died down, we put our vegetables and the fish on the coals. While we were waiting for everything to cook, we opened the beer, Coca-Cola, and Diet Pepsi. After spending two days in hot weather, those icy drinks were just what we needed.

Dan cooked all the fish, so we would be able to have it in jambalaya the next night. The pike had a lot of bones but was quite tasty, and along with the vegetables, we had an enjoyable dinner. As we ate, a river otter swam by about 20 ft (6 m) from shore.

By 7:45 p.m. we were on the river again. We hoped to get in another two or three hours before we found a camp spot for the night. The air was hot and still, and we were continuing to sweat heavily under our shirts and life jackets. We passed a tundra swan swimming along the north bank, and later, two bald eagles studied us as we paddled through their breeding area.

After a couple of hours, we began looking for a camp spot, but the shoreline was either steep, eroding, or muddy. In our third hour of paddling, with little promise of finding an adequate landing, we paddled to the opposite side of the river. Each spot that looked encouraging from a distance turned out to be either muddy or strewn with boulders. A large formation of clouds began blocking the sun, and at 11:45 p.m., a light rain began to fall. We hoped the rain would shoo away the mosquitoes, which had been with us since dinner, but the rain didn't seem to bother them. In fact, the number of mosquitoes increased, and they became more aggressive as the sun dipped toward the horizon. The rain subsided shortly after it began, so any hope that it would help us was lost anyway. My mosquito head net was buried in my dry bag, so I put on an extra layer of Jungle Juice. The pests kept hitting my face, but they didn't stay long enough to drill into my skin.

In my research I had learned about Brownings Landing. I knew we were a long way from there, and the sun had set, but I mentioned to Dan that since we had gone this far and hadn't found a place to camp, maybe we should just plod on to Brownings Landing. He made a less-than-positive comment that made me laugh, and we continued on.

The storm clouds were drifting away, which was a good sign, but it was so dark it was hard to see the shore. We decided to return to the north side since we were striking out to the south. The Noels had been forced to camp somewhere close by when the wind came up and wound up camping in mud—something we weren't interested in doing. The mosquitoes kept attacking my face, which was annoying. Dan was wearing his head net, and from my seat in the stern, it looked like he had an Afro as a thick swarm of mosquitoes circled his head.

The north shore wasn't any better, so we crossed the river again. I began thinking about Sue, hoping she wasn't worried about me. I was glad she didn't know we were paddling after midnight, in the dark, exhausted, and a bit discouraged. I had to put the thought of lying on our soft queen-size bed out of my mind.

Phil and Don were quite a ways back, and in the darkness, I wasn't sure they could see us. I called out to them but didn't hear a response. In the distance ahead, Dan spotted a light and thought it might be a barge or the Coast Guard ship *Dumit*. As we came closer, we concluded it was on one of the navigation buoys placed by the Coast Guard. Through the dark a long distance ahead, we saw what looked like a sandy beach. I didn't get my hopes up because I believed we were still a long way from Brownings Landing. We had already seen more than a dozen likely spots that ended in disappointment. With little optimism, we turned toward the hope of a paradise we didn't expect to find. As tired as I was, I was looking forward to being inside my tent—more to be away from the mosquitos than to sleep.

We paddled straight toward the beach, which looked better the closer we came. Perhaps it wasn't just a mirage. We landed at about 1:30 a.m. and found a flat sandy spot where others had camped. I walked away from the beach and saw an old boat and several cabins. Suddenly, I realized where we were. Fortunately, Phil and Don had spotted us. "Welcome to Brownings Landing!" I yelled as they arrived.

"How did you find this place?" Phil asked as he climbed ashore. His belief in my skills as a navigator were more than I deserved. I had been reading topographical maps since I was a kid and had a summer job while I was in college plotting aerial photos on maps for the Forest Inventory Section of the Washington State Department of Natural Resources. However, trying to follow the topography in the dark with a map with small light-colored lines and writing was nearly impossible. I had to admit that getting us to Brownings Landing was as much luck as skill.

I couldn't get my tent up fast enough. The mosquitoes that had followed us on the river had joined their relatives on the beach. However, even though it was nearly morning, and the northern sun was about to rise, I had to take time for a shot of Yukon Jack with my three compadres.

43.7 mi (70.3 km) traveled today – 78.2 mi (125.8 km) overall

Campsite location: N61°17'47.5" W119°47'59.4"

FIVE
Jean Marie River

"May your footsteps leave only friends behind." – Frederic M. Perrin (linguist and author) in Rella Two Trees - The Money Chiefs

Monday, June 19, 2006 – Brownings Landing to Jean Marie River

I woke up at 7:00 a.m. and checked my GPS for our location, confirming we had landed at Brownings Landing, now known as Browning Point. In the 1960s, Jack Browning and his family started a sawmill operation there. Some records show that in the late 1700s, a small community was located there and perhaps the first fur-trading post on the Mackenzie River.

The wind that we needed the day before to keep the mosquitoes at bay arrived that morning. Don and I had pulled the canoes up on the sandy shore when we landed, but the wind was creating waves high enough that they were slapping the sides and causing spray to get inside. We had been in such a hurry to get our tents out at 1:30 in the morning that we had left the gear in disarray. I pulled the canoes up the beach, took out some of the gear, and began reorganizing and reloading.

I stripped down and waded into the ice-cold river to take a quick sponge bath—very quick! After putting on clean underwear and a shirt, Dan and I walked up to check out a cabin we had seen from the river as we were approaching the landing. We found a large grassy area with a small cabin under construction, started a long time ago but never finished. Near the back of the meadow were two old cabins, so we walked over to explore the old structures. One looked to be in useful condition, and the other was used for storage, a generator visible through the open door.

When we returned, Phil and Don were using the satellite phone. I called Sue and left a message on her voicemail. We had brought the satellite phone with us at the insistence of Phil's wife, Kathy, and with further urging from the other wives. I had to admit, I was happy to have that link to the outside world.

A storm was brewing upriver to the east as we began paddling downstream. We stayed close to the left bank to avoid lightning as the storm began to rumble in the distance. We didn't want to be a lightning rod in the middle of the wide, flat river.

Within half an hour, rain began to fall, so we stopped to put on our raincoats and spray covers on the canoes. Don had made the covers the previous spring in anticipation of rain and rough water. This was the first real rain so far, so it was a good time to test the spray covers and our rain gear. The rain increased as we paddled past a small island about 5 mi (8 km) into our day, and the river began to narrow to one-sixth the width it was at Brownings Landing. As the river narrowed, the speed of the current increased—a welcome change after two days of still water.

We heard a roar ahead and anticipated rapids, but as we approached, we realized it was only a Coast Guard buoy marking the channel and fighting against the swift current. The rain continued to fall as bald eagles watched us from the trees along the riverbank. We stopped twice to stretch our legs and snack on nuts, crackers, cheese, and sausage. We each brought our own food for breakfast, lunch, and snacks but cooked together for dinners. Dan and I provided dinner every other night, and Phil and Don were responsible for the other nights. When we had the makings for foil dinners, we skipped the planned menu.

It was becoming apparent that we were truly in the wilderness because we hadn't seen another human in two days. At 5:30 p.m. we reached the village of Jean Marie River, population fifty, mostly Aboriginal. I hadn't expected to reach the village that day, but the swift current propelled us much faster than the slow-moving water of Mills Lake. We pulled our canoes up the steep bank at the edge of town, and Dan and I walked through a cluster of homes, looking for a phone we could use to report our arrival to the RCMP. We asked a very nice woman if she could direct us to a telephone. She told us there was a phone "at the office," but it was closed. When we explained the purpose of our call, she pulled out her cell phone and dialed the number before handing the phone to me.

After I reported our arrival, I asked if she could recommend a location where we could pitch our tents. She said we could camp anywhere down on the riverbank. After thanking her for the help, we located a large grassy area where we pitched the Tundra tent and our individual tents. We were almost out of drinking water, so I walked back up to the cluster of homes, saw the same woman, and asked where we might find some drinking water. She went inside her home and came out with several bottles of water. "The water in town is no good because of the runoff," she said. "We don't drink it." Everyone we had met since we arrived in Hay River had been very gracious. I was feeling very good about the expedition.

I crawled into my tent at about 9:30 p.m., hearing the sound of three men building a flat-bottom scow close to the house where we made our phone call. As I was settling in, I heard a barge on the river, so I crawled out to see if it might be the one transporting the truck. I was used to barges being pulled in the waters of Puget Sound near our home and in British Columbia, where we have a cabin on Hardy Island north of Vancouver. On the river the barges are pushed rather than pulled, giving the tugboats more control in the current. I hadn't thought to grab my camera, but Dan was better prepared than me and snapped a few shots. The barge was enormous and seemed to fill the river in front of us. Our truck was not aboard.

I went to sleep to the sound of yapping dogs staked not far from our camp.

34.9 mi (56.2 km) traveled today – 113.1 mi (182 km) overall

Campsite location: N61°31'58.5" W120°37'48.3"

SIX
Fort Simpson

"Clouds of insects danced and buzzed in the golden autumn light, and the air was full of the piping of the song-birds. Long, glinting dragonflies shot across the path, or hung tremulous with gauzy wings and gleaming bodies." – Arthur Conan Doyle

Tuesday, June 20, 2006 – Jean Marie River to Fort Simpson

I woke up at around 6:00 a.m. and read for an hour. One of the nice things about being in the Arctic in the summer is the many hours of sunshine. I could read when I went to bed as well as when I woke up without having to use a headlamp. At 7:00 a.m. I stuffed my sleeping bag into its stuff sack and rolled the air out of my Thermarest mattress. I seemed to be the only one up as I went to the Tundra tent to save some of the water that usually collects on top when it's been raining. Because of the water shortage in Jean Marie River, I hoped to collect some water from the tent for washing. Apparently, none of the sprinkles overnight had collected on the tent, so I came up empty.

Inside, a number of mosquitoes were dancing on the netting, so I pulled out my handy zapper and began taking revenge. The loud snap as each one was incinerated was loud enough to wake the others, but I didn't hear any movement. Shortly, Don walked into camp. After waking up at 6:00 a.m., he explained, he had dumped the water from the tent and walked into the village.

When Dan got up, he and I walked up to the Déné band office. On the way we met a guy named Raymond, who had shot a moose the day before. He had taken a short break from preparing the meat for the smoker and stepped over to say hello. While we were talking to him, the *Noweta* passed the village on its way downriver.

The Déné Nation comprises a large section of land in the interior of Western Canada, not including the Pacific Coastal areas and the northernmost areas along the coast of the Arctic Ocean. The Déné band office is the center of each community. It's where community business is done and where there is a focus on traditions, values, and beliefs. Their mission includes using and protecting the natural resources, so they will be available for present and future generations.

We were given permission to use the office phone to call home. Sue was at our son John's home, taking care of our grandson, Luke. She also had our grandson, Nathaniel (Reed's son), with her. Everything was well on the home front, and I was able to assure her that all was well on the river too.

When we inquired about the weather, we were provided a printout of the forecast that indicated the rain would subside during the day, and the next day would be partly cloudy. Beyond that we could expect four days of sunshine, a welcome discovery because the rain was a bit discouraging.

In the office we met Angus Sanchez, a resident of Jean Marie River. Apparently, everyone in the village was aware of our presence. Angus was a guide, taking visitors on fishing and sightseeing excursions from Fort Simpson. We asked about fishing on the river, and he gave us tips on catching walleye and northern pike. We told him about our big pike, but after hearing about his fishing experiences, it didn't seem so gigantic anymore. He said he would be going to Fort Simpson that evening and leading excursions for the next few days. We learned that the next day was Aboriginal Day, and there would be celebrations and a canoe race there.

We returned to the Tundra tent along with a cloud of mosquitoes. Angus stopped by and brought us two lures that he said were good for catching walleye. He stayed, and we talked more about fishing and the river. I enjoyed his slow, gentle nature. He used few words to express himself and spent as much time listening as talking. When he laughed, his entire face lit up. He also seemed very wise for his age, which I estimated to be between thirty and thirty-five.

Dan, Phil, and I walked back to the band office to get water. The woman who gave us the forecast said the water at the office came from the Jean Marie River and had been treated. While we were filling our containers, we met George Bell, who was working in the office and had come out to meet us. George was

Caucasian and was married to a Déné woman from Jean Marie River. He was a financial consultant and did work for the Déné Band. He had paddled portions of the Mackenzie and shared valuable information about the approach to the Ramparts, rapids we would be paddling through far downriver.

When we returned to the Tundra tent, Angus joined us again. He stayed while we packed and loaded our canoes in a downpour. He recommended we stop for lunch at Rabbitskin River where there was a grassy area with a picnic table and a fire ring. As we left at high noon, I yelled to him to look us up in Fort Simpson, and I'd buy him a beer.

A half mile beyond Jean Marie River, the current increased, and we quickly passed Spence River where the Noel family camped. The rain began to decrease, and we felt optimistic that we could reach Fort Simpson in about six hours.

At 3:00 p.m. we arrived at Rabbitskin River. We pulled along the shore and saw a trail leading up the high bank to a grassy area. There was no beach between the river and the incline, and it was difficult to climb out of the canoes. We tied the bow and stern lines to bushes and kept the canoes floating in the river as we climbed the bank, carrying our lunches to the flat above. The spot was every bit as splendid as Angus had described. There were two tables, a firepit, an outhouse, and several pots and pans. At the back were two well-built cabins.

As we walked through the grass, thousands of mosquitoes rose up and began attacking us. We put on our head nets and tried to get our food under the net without bringing in the vicious pests. That proved to be nearly impossible, and we began talking about heading back onto the water to eat our lunch on the move. Suddenly, we were attacked by dragonflies, which hit our head nets, shoulders, and arms. I'd never been attacked by a dragonfly before and was mystified until I realized they weren't attacking us; they were attacking the mosquitoes. Within minutes, the mosquitoes were gone. We took off our head nets and finished our lunch in peace. From that point on, we were glad to have dragonflies nearby.

When we came alongside Green Island, we heard the sound of a motorboat. It was quite a distance upstream, but when it came closer, we recognized Angus and two of his friends on their way to Fort Simpson. One of his friends said the water around Fort Simpson was so high it would be impossible to camp near town. He explained that Fort Simpson was built on an island and suggested we try the boat launch, past the town at the far end of the island. Soon they were on their way, and we paddled on to Martin Island, where we originally planned to camp, but the banks were steep, and the trees on the flat above were close together with brush between. We surmised that later in the summer when the river receded, the island could be a reasonable site for a camp, but not that day.

From Martin Island we could see the buildings of Fort Simpson on the left side of the river, just beyond where the Liard River entered the Mackenzie. We had heard of flooding up the Liard River, but the amount of debris being carried down was staggering. Logs, root systems, branches, and mud were streaming into the Mackenzie. Angus had recommended we stay to the left side of the Mackenzie to minimize the push of the Liard's current. We stayed as far left as possible and paddled right into the mess, dodging logs and other debris, digging our paddles deep into the chocolate-brown water. The Mackenzie was laden with silt, but there was a clear delineation between the lighter water of the big river and that of the Liard.

During our crossing we kept the bow facing to the left to keep the Liard from pushing us away from town. We aimed for the teepee-like structure at the upriver end of the island, built for the visit of Pope John Paul II on September 20, 1987. Despite the report of the conditions from Angus and his friends, we stayed close to shore, looking for possible locations to land close to town. We passed homes and floatplanes tied to docks, but the riverbank was steep, and the water was high.

We passed a Déné man sitting on a bench beside the river and asked him if the boat launch was close. He pointed downriver but said a better place to camp was farther down. We hoped to visit the town and find a restaurant for dinner, so we stopped at the boat launch to appraise conditions for a camp. Finding it unsatisfactory, we paddled farther down to find the recommended site. Not far past the boat launch, we found an opening in the brush and went ashore. There was a cleared area and a road leading, we believed, to town. It was apparent the area had recently been flooded, but we found some dryer areas to pitch our tents. We knew it was our last chance if we wanted to visit the town because we had reached the end of the island. If it rained, we would have a mess because we were camping on dried mud.

After pitching our tents, Dan and I walked up the road to see if there was a KFC or a pizza joint where we could have dinner and a beer. An RCMP car passed us, heading toward our camp. When he came back, we flagged him down, explained our situation, and asked if we could check in with him. He wrote down our information and said he would pass it on to Hay River. We told him where we were headed, and he broke the bad news that all the restaurants were closed, though we might be able to get a sandwich at a place called T.J.'s Market.

After a walk of over a mile, we entered T.J's and found that the only sandwiches were frozen and needed to be heated in a microwave. The young Déné woman behind the counter confirmed what the RCMP officer had said, that no restaurants were open because of the Aboriginal Day celebrations. She was about to close and offered us four free Little Smokies that had to be disposed of anyway. We chatted with her for a few minutes and learned she was a theater apprentice in Winnipeg and had just returned home the previous week.

We used a phone in the store to call home. I spoke to Sue, the second time that day, and learned that little Luke had fallen and bruised his mouth. Other than that, all was well. Dan called his son and found out his daughter-in-law was expecting a boy—they already had a girl. Such connections with home were important, being that we were so far away and isolated most of the time. We left T.J.s with the hot Little Smokies and a two-liter bottle of Coca-Cola that cost almost five dollars. Dan and I ate our Little Smokies on the way back to camp. Phil and Don were very happy with the Smokies and Coke.

40.4 mi (65.0 km) traveled today – 153.5 mi (247 km) overall

Campsite location: N61°52'55.1" W121°23'45.0"

SEVEN
Wrigley Ferry

"Good decisions come from experience. Experience comes from making bad decisions." – Mark Twain

Wednesday, June 21, 2006 – Fort Simpson to the Wrigley Ferry Crossing

By 9:30 a.m. we were on our way again, happy to be away from our muddy camp just downriver from Fort Simpson. We were disappointed we weren't able to spend some time in town to enjoy the Aboriginal Day celebrations, but we were anxious to move along while the weather held. Our goal for the day was to reach the Wrigley Ferry Crossing, a little more than 43 mi (69 km) downriver. If the current continued at the present rate, it was doable.

After two and a half hours of paddling, we stopped on the second of two small islands, about 10 mi (16 km) downriver. I was hoping to reach Trail River, but Dan was anxious to stop. He knows only one speed, full-tilt ahead. He hadn't been sleeping well and couldn't seem to rebound.

The beach was strewn with boulders and gravel. It was very unstable, and when we walked, the boulders slid out from under our feet. As Phil stepped out of his canoe into the water, a boulder rolled under his feet. One foot went in deep enough that water flowed into his boot. He shared his frustration with some colorful language, climbed out of the water, and joined us farther up on shore. We ate a quick lunch and pumped drinking water from the edge of the river. The water from the Liard had not mixed with the water along the island, which was relatively clear, so we didn't need to worry about silt clogging the filter.

We paddled on and made our next stop a short distance from the Trail River. Some cabins were on the flat above a steep bank, and a log cabin was under construction. We secured the canoes to a log along the bank and climbed up what looked like an animal trail. I was happy to find a two-hole outhouse, which came in handy. A sprinkle of rain and a steady wind kept the mosquitoes at bay. After a good half-hour rest, we continued our journey.

From shore we could see one of the Coast Guard buoys struggling to stay afloat in the fast-moving water. Although we preferred to stay close to shore, the swift water out near the buoy enticed us to paddle out where we could move faster. We paddled past Trail River and agreed we had made a good decision stopping on the little island to rest because there was no bank visible with the edge of the river high up into the brush.

We began to see more massive chunks of ice along the shoreline. At 4:45 p.m., in the distance we saw a small white speck in the middle of the river, which turned out to be the Wrigley Ferry crossing from the left bank to the right bank. By 5:30 p.m. we arrived at the landing on the right bank, where the ferry was waiting for cars. Phil and Don arrived, and we discussed whether we should move on and hope to find a better camp spot or land by the ferry to see if there was potential there. It seemed that each of us had a different opinion. I insisted we at least have a look, remembering our long night on Mills Lake.

We paddled just past the ferry, caught a back eddy, and pulled ashore. The Noels had camped there, but there was no sign of a campsite and no potential for us to make camp because the shoreline had been badly torn up by the spring ice flow and high water. From the river I saw a cleared area about 200 ft (61 m) up the road and to the left. A couple of deckhands came over to talk to us, and I asked them about the area up the road. One of them, named Blair, said he thought it would be a good place to camp. The other, Henry Hardisty, started playing a twelve-string Yamaha Guitar. They offered us coffee and allowed us to fill our water bottles from their tank on the ferry.

The Wrigley ferry is part of the highway system that links Fort Simpson and the village of Wrigley, which are 137 mi (220.5 km) apart. That section of road is called the Heritage Route and was completed in 1994. It is part of Highway 1, which begins in Grimshaw, Alberta, and ends at Wrigley. The original plan was to continue northward and to connect with the Dempster Highway, which links Inuvik with towns in the Yukon. A winter road continues from Wrigley across the frozen land to Norman Wells, Fort Good Hope, and Colville Lake.

The road made for easy walking, and we discovered the cleared area was a gravel pit used to store the rock that would be used to repair the ferry landing as the current worked to tear it apart. I expected there was a loader on the other side of the river, used to maintain both landings. An ample supply of gravel was piled up in the pit, waiting until the water subsided or when the landing needed improvement.

A flat gravel area in the pit was better than any of our other campsites so far, with the exception of Brownings Landing. We all agreed it was an excellent camp spot but a long way from our canoes and gear. We decided to carry everything up, so we would have our gear handy and our canoes within sight. We set up all the tents and erected a clothesline to dry our wet clothing and other gear.

Don cooked dinner. He's an avid backpacker and had perfected a way of drying and packaging foods for hiking trips that required keeping weight to a minimum. His specialty that night was chicken and stuffing along with bannock and hot chocolate. The food was appetizing, but the portions were small. Apparently, Don's success in keeping his backpack light was due partly to limiting the amount of food for each meal.

During the night I was awakened by a racket down at the landing that turned out to be a group of men launching a boat. I was pleased we had carried our canoes a good distance away from the noise of vehicles arriving and departing as well as the sounds of the ferry scraping gravel as it landed on the beach. The noise lasted only a short time, and I slept well the remainder of the night.

43.9 mi (70.7 km) traveled today – 197.4 mi (317.7 km) overall

Campsite location: N61°08'49.8" W122°31'38"

EIGHT
Nahanni River

"A true leader has the confidence to stand alone, the courage to make tough decisions, and the compassion to listen to the needs of others. He does not set out to be a leader, but becomes one by the equality of his actions and the integrity of his intent." – Douglas MacArthur

Thursday, June 22, 2006 – Wrigley
Crossing to the Nahanni River

I woke up around 6:30 a.m. and read for an hour before I crawled out of the tent. I unsnapped my dew-soaked tent fly and hung it on the clothesline we had put up the night before.

In the distance I heard a truck winding its way along the gravel highway. A pilot car soon arrived, followed by a large truck that was carrying a bulldozer. Dan, Phil, Don, and I walked down to the ferry landing as two men, Kevin and Devin, climbed out of the truck. Phil introduced himself, and the rest of us did the same. They explained that they had a contract to work on the gravel road to Wrigley. They knew the area well and provided us with important information including a couple of good campsites: one just before the Willowlake River and another at River Between Two Mountains. They said the store in Wrigley would be open between 10:00 a.m. and 6:00 p.m. and closed for an hour during lunch. Devin advised us not to stay in the village, "Some of these people have been in the bush too long—they come out with guns and knives." They suggested we camp before Wrigley because afterward the cliffs were too steep for a long way.

PERSEVERANCE

After breakfast we carried our canoes and gear down to the ferry landing, which took a long time because of how far we were from the river. By 10:50 a.m. we were on the river again. The sun came out, and only a few wispy clouds were on the southern horizon. The river was wide and swift with many islands to navigate around.

Dan and I fell into a kind of unconscious rhythm, paddling in unison and taking in the area's rustic beauty. I was feeling confident and happy, doing something I had dreamed about for decades. I was taking a break from my busy existence of educational consulting, but the solitude of our wilderness experience led me to reflect on the work I had been doing for the past five years.

After I retired as an elementary school principal, I worked in the Educational Leadership department at City University of Seattle as a field supervisor of principal interns. My philosophy of leadership began to develop when I was a teacher as I observed principals and other school administrators. Those who were successful didn't see themselves as "the boss" but as facilitators of learning. They focused on the core mission and developed leadership strategies to reach that mission. I believe this to be true of any successful leader, whether a business leader, a military officer, or an educational leader. The strength of any group or organization comes from the members, working together to solve problems and to move the organization toward its goals. A leader works with the members to clarify those goals, provide valuable information, and to bring about a consensus around major efforts toward reaching those goals. A leader must build the group's capacity to make quality decisions independently as well as in small and large groups that move the group closer to their ultimate goal. In any organization, leaders come and go, and if anyone thinks they are indispensable, they are kidding themselves. Now that I am no longer a principal, part of my second career is helping develop successful principals. I tell my interns that anyone can be a boss, but being a leader takes, among other things, finesse, organization, good communication skills, and foremost, the ability to listen. There is a time for direct action, but if the leader isn't around at that time, other members of the organization must be able to step up and make decisions. The quality of those decisions is intimately related to the leader's modeling and practices.

My leadership of this expedition was rooted in a collaborative effort that included ideas from each one of us in the planning stages. On the river, we all knew our goal, we trusted each other's skills and knowledge, and we made major decisions by listening to others and making compromises where compromises made sense. I felt a sense of responsibility for each member of the group because I was the one who had suggested that river. On the river I listened carefully and observed how each individual was progressing, when they needed a break, how strong they felt each day, and how long we should paddle. I think the others were doing the same because no one seemed to be out for himself.

Our late start that morning resulted in another late stop for lunch. We found a good location to pull ashore, stretch our backs, and dig into our dry bags for our crackers, cheese, and sausage. We sat on the riverbank eating our lunch and watching the bees as they moved from one blue flower to another. A butterfly joined them, and one flew to my water bottle and feasted on the droplets of lemonade on the edge. Almost no mosquitoes bothered us at that location, perhaps due to our friends, the dragonflies, circulating around us.

We were back on the river by 2:00 p.m., paddling on the south side of a series of islands, approaching the confluence of the North Nahanni River and the Mackenzie. The North Nahanni begins in the Nahanni National Park Reserve, a unique area that includes granite spires, sandstone arches, mineral pools, hot springs, raging rivers, and spectacular canyons. One of the largest falls in Canada is Virginia Falls on the South Nahanni River, dropping 315 ft (96 m), almost twice the height of Niagara Falls. The terrain began to change as we approached the North Nahanni. Mt. Nahanni towered above us at an elevation of 4,038 ft (1,231 m). The elevation of the river at that location was a little over 500 ft (about 150 m). We were leaving behind a landscape of flat marshland, and the Camsell Mountain Range was straight ahead with steep exposed rock and horizontal striations.

At 4:45 p.m. we reached the waters of the North Nahanni River, laden with silt even denser than the Liard River. Heavy rain and melting snow in the mountains was rushing down the creeks, tearing at the banks and turning the Nahanni into a stew of mud and plant life. The Mackenzie took a dogleg turn north, and we paddled along the left side and through a narrow passage behind an island. We spied a sandy bank with enough flat space above to make camp, so we pulled in for the night. The site was not great, but thunderclouds were forming, and we were tired of paddling and ready for a long rest. We even decided to skip dinner and snack on crackers, cheese, and summer sausage. I lay down and took a nap until about 8:00 p.m.

PERSEVERANCE

Finding suitable water to filter had been a constant challenge. My large pump filter could fill a five-gallon container in just a few minutes as long as the water was free of silt. In most places the Mackenzie was so full of sediment that we didn't even consider pumping from the river. Small streams entering the river were our best option, but most came from stagnant, swampy areas and were the color of coffee. Our filters kept out bacteria, so if we could find a stream with clear water, we stopped to pump it through the filters and into our containers. We were getting low on water, so our plan for the next day was to paddle close to the shore and look for suitable water.

Phil rigged up the sun shower on a tripod of driftwood poles, so we were able to take showers. The sun shower was a big plastic bag that we filled with water. The front of the bag was clear plastic, and the back was black. The sun's ray projected through the clear plastic and the water and were absorbed by the black plastic panel, heating the water to temperatures that varied between lukewarm and very hot, depending on the intensity of the sun and amount of time exposed. Since we weren't drinking that water, we weren't as concerned about the quality as long as it wasn't loaded with silt. After almost a week of sponge baths, the warm shower was a welcome change.

29.5 mi (47.5 km) traveled today – 226.9 mi (365.2 km) overall

Campsite location: N62°16'22.7" W123°23'32.5"

NINE
Willowlake River

"If you want to see the sunshine, you have to weather the storm." – Frank Lane

Friday, June 23, 2006 – Nahanni River to Willowlake River

A heavy downpour began shortly after 6:30 a.m. as I was about to get up. I decided to wait it out and fell back asleep. An hour later the rain had stopped, and I figured it was time to crawl out. I looked through the netting and into the vestibule to see a mass of mosquitoes under the cover of the tent fly, out of the rain. I lit a mosquito coil and slipped it through the zipper and into the vestibule. The smoke soon drove out most of the mosquitoes. I rolled up my sleeping bag and Thermarest and headed to the Tundra tent.

We could hear geese honking throughout the early morning, and a swan across the river added its own refrain as it splashed into the river. The Noels paddled 48 mi (77 km) after leaving that location. We weren't sure if they put in an extra-long day or the river had become swifter. The river had turned north, and we would be paddling parallel to the Camsell Mountain Range, expecting stunning scenery. Based on the information from Kevin and Devin (back at the Wrigley Crossing), Willowlake River, some 30 mi (48 km) ahead, had a good camping area. River Between Two Mountains was another option, but it was 48 mi (77 km) ahead.

We were on the river by 10:00 a.m., having spent the night at a marginal but sufficient campsite. We had kept our canoes floating overnight in the river because there was no beach, and the bank was too steep to bring them up to our camp. We tied the painters, bow and stern, securely to scrubby willows on the riverbank. By morning the canoes were on a beach about 3 ft (0.9 m) from the river. We estimated the river had dropped about a foot overnight. It was the second day we had noticed a significant drop, a good omen.

As we paddled around the island, we saw a red buoy stationed close to the mainland. The water was moving swiftly there, but it didn't appear to be a good location for a barge. Perhaps the swift current had moved it from its moorage in the center of the river.

Two hours later we landed on an island just past Root River. More muddy beaches were exposed, and in places, there was 40 ft (12 m) or more of beach between the river and the bank. The ice had scoured the bank in many places, forcing mud, saplings, and exposed roots onto the newly exposed beach.

It felt good to be out of the canoe, walking and stretching our muscles. Dan was rummaging around in the canoe, looking for his sausage, when Phil saw Dan's paddle slip off the canoe and into the water. It was very uncharacteristic of Dan not to stow the paddle securely, but exhaustion is an enemy we needed to be constantly aware of. I've done the same thing but was lucky not to lose the paddle. I ran downriver and was able to guide the paddle to shore with a long stick. It was a reminder for all of us. If we had lost the paddle, we would need to use our only spare and would be in a difficult situation if we lost another.

We ate lunch and decided to paddle to Willowlake River, about 19 mi (31 km) downriver, cook our dinner, and decide if we wanted to camp there or move on. Clouds were forming over the Nahanni Range, and a thunderstorm was sure to follow. Similar clouds were forming ahead of us. The temperature was 85°F (30°C). A breeze would have been welcome, but there was nothing to cause a ripple on the river other than swirls made by the current.

The wind came up in the afternoon, but it was more than we expected, and it came up so fast that it surprised us. Fortunately, we weren't out in the middle of the river, and we paddled close to shore for the next couple of hours, battling the waves and the wind and getting a spray of water in the canoe. I had been somewhat complacent about the weather, not keeping a close eye on the clouds or an staying alert for choppy water ahead or behind us. It was surreal how fast the chop came at us, from hundreds of feet away in a matter of seconds.

The wind eventually died down as we cruised on the east side of 15-mile-long (24-km) McGern Island. A thunderstorm was brewing, and it looked like it would bring strong winds, so we dug our paddles deep and fast and headed for a gravel beach strewn with boulders to our right.

When we landed at 3:00 p.m., the water was relatively calm. In the distance, perhaps two miles away, black clouds were dropping sheets of rain, and they were moving our way. Minutes later the water changed from placid to rough to wild. Large waves crashed onto the shore, reaching our canoe, which we had secured several feet from the river. We raced to the canoes and brought them several yards higher, so they wouldn't be smashed on the boulders. These were the types of waves we would see on a stormy day in Jervis Inlet, British Columbia, with the wind building several miles up the fjord, turning the surface of the water dark and then arriving with tumultuous fury. It was a reminder to keep our eyes on the sky ahead and not be caught too far from shore farther downriver where the width was two or three times wider than it was at that point.

Sprinkles followed by heavy rain came with the wind, and I pulled out a red nylon tarp. The four of us sat on a log and held the tarp above our heads until the deluge ended forty-five minutes later. At 5:00 p.m. the wind began to subside but not enough for us to safely enter the river. We hadn't yet put on the spray skirts Don had made and decided that would be a good time to finish the ties that we would use to attach the skirt to the canoe. We all agreed that the River Between Two Mountains was out of the question, and we weren't sure we could make it to Willowlake River in such conditions.

By 5:30 p.m. the wind had died down enough that we continued on, hugging the shoreline in case it got worse. Dan and I took the lead, and once we felt comfortable that we could handle the wave action, we moved farther out into the river where the current was moving about twice the speed it was along the shore. I was happy with the way my Mad River Revelation handled in the rough water. Dan concurred that we had the right canoe for the trip.

It was near 7:00 p.m. when we reached the camp that Kevin and Devin recommended. We hadn't reached Willowlake River yet, but we could see it was just beyond the campsite. A narrow gravel road led down to the river from a grassy area. I saw the poles for the teepees and knew we had reached our destination.

Dan flagged down Phil and Don, who turned quickly to shore and joined us. The area appeared ideal for a camp with a fire ring and flat ground for our tents. However, our nemesis, the mosquitoes, were in full attack mode. We lathered up with Jungle Juice, started a fire, and prepared foil dinners. When the coals were ready, we laid our dinners down and began our twenty-five-minute countdown. If the foil is tight enough, you won't smell the food cooking because the steam can't escape into the air, but that night the delicious smell of potatoes, carrots, cabbage, and sausage filled the air. When it was time to pull our dinners from the coals, I discovered my foil pouch was the one that wasn't sealed tightly. Some of the juices had leaked out, and there was a burnt crust on most of the food. That didn't deter me from digging in and enjoying a feast that we had all earned by our efforts in a challenging environment

Throughout the evening we heard dogs barking and assumed someone was camped close by. By 10:00 p.m. we toasted the fine day with a shot of Yukon Jack and then retreated to our tents to clear out the mosquitoes and have a restful night.

Every night until that night, it took a long time before I could slip into my sleeping bag because of the heat. That night I was able to climb in immediately. We were on our way to the Arctic Circle and beyond—moving away from the heat and into a cooler environment, something we were prepared for and looking forward to!

31.8 mi (51.2 km) traveled today – 258.7 mi (416.4 km) overall

Campsite location: N62°41'33" W123°07'51"

TEN
Wrigley

"May your footsteps leave only friends behind." – Frederic M. Perrin, in Rella Two Trees - The Money Chiefs

Saturday, June 24, 2006 – Willowlake River to Wrigley

I woke up in the middle of the night to a light rain hitting my tent fly. It lasted only a few minutes, but it brought cooler weather, and it was the coldest night yet. I went right back to sleep until around 5:30 a.m. I read a while and then dozed as the mosquitoes serenaded me. The dogs that were barking the previous night started again. When the sun hit my tent, it warmed up considerably. It also brought out more mosquitoes, and I dreaded the race between my tent and the Tundra tent.

At 7:00 a.m. I heard Dan and Don talking in their tent and decided it was time to lather up with Jungle Juice and make my escape to the shelter of the big tent and breakfast.

After breakfast we broke camp, carried our gear down to the canoes, loaded up, and shoved off. In less than a minute of paddling, Willowlake River came into view. Its water was clear, a big change from the Mackenzie and its tributaries up to that point. We saw several cabins in a grassy area across the Willowlake River and heard dogs barking near the cabins. A 20-foot (6 m) bank stretched from a few hundred feet up the Willowlake, down and around a point, and then about a half mile down the MacKenzie.

A small damaged floating dock was attached to the far shore. We paddled across the mouth of the Willowlake and tied up to the dock to pump that clear water into our containers. Just as we were about to begin, a man named Robert Hardisty appeared on the bank above and came down to meet us. He saw that we were collecting water and advised us against it because of mining upriver that was putting contaminants into the river. He said they collected rainwater from their roof, and we could fill our containers there.

We secured our canoes and followed him up a narrow trail to the plateau above and to his home. While walking to the cabins, we learned that Robert was a cousin of Henry Hardisty, the guitar-playing deckhand on the ferry at Wrigley Crossing. There were three houses on the site and a teepee at the edge of the bank in front of the houses with the front third open and a campfire burning inside. Robert said they closed the teepee tight when they smoked meat. We also met a woman named Rita Betsedea, whom he introduced as his "common-law wife." Robert and Rita had been living there for five years. Robert trapped in the winter, using his sled and dog team to tend to his traps. He trapped lynx, martins, beavers, minks, wolverine, and sometimes fishers. It was bad luck, he said, to club an animal caught in a trap. Robert described spending nights out on the trail under a tarp and next to a fire to keep warm.

Standing in the doorway of a light-blue house was an elderly gentleman, an uncle to Robert. His name was Victor Pauncha-Boot, and he was eighty-nine years old. He and his brothers had lived on that point all their lives. Two of his brothers were buried across the river on McGern Island, directly across from their homes. Robert pointed out the grave sites in the distance, bordered by a picket fence. The other brother, "Joah" George Boot, was buried in the woods not far from the houses. Joah was a legendary elder of the Deh Cho people who came to trap at that site in 1934.

The wind picked up as we chatted with Robert and Rita, so we were in no hurry to return to the river. Robert brought out some of his furs, including a large lynx and three martins. He said Willowlake River is called "Xahndah" in the Déné language (pronounced "honda,"), which means "goose nest." With the wind picking up and the threat of rain, we were thankful that Robert and Rita were so gracious in welcoming us to their home. Robert told us about a book titled *Trapping is my Life* by John Tetso (also spelled Tsetso), a Déné man who at one time lived at that site.

Robert began making bannock in a cast-iron frying pan on his campfire. He gave us his recipe of one cup of flour, one tablespoon of baking powder, sugar, raisins, egg, and milk. We sat under cover in the teepee as the rain began to fall. The smoke made our eyes tear up, but at least we were dry, and we were intrigued by Robert's stories.

His tales included his own experiences in the bush but also the folklore of the Déné community, passed down by word of mouth from generation to generation. He told us how the Mackenzie River was formed by a giant who rolled a big ball of dried meat down the valley. Wherever a piece of meat fell off the ball was a good hunting place. Lakes were formed when the giant was chasing beavers and scooped out the mud where the beavers had burrowed underground. There was a place downriver where a seam of coal had been ablaze for centuries, and the local belief was that it was burning beaver grease from the giant beavers. He told us the Nahanni Range and the Camsell Range were formed by a giant beaver.

A Canadian flag was flying on the point. Robert said that George, one of Victor's brothers, had flown an American flag during the Iraq war. Robert told him they might send a missile after him. The next day, the Canadian flag was flying in its place.

Victor did not speak English. He spoke the Aboriginal language of the area, South Slavey. I asked Rita if I could take a picture of Victor, and she agreed. But when I went to take the picture, Victor put his hand in front of his face. "He thinks you are trying to steal a part of him," Robert said.

When the bannock was cooked, Robert gave us each a piece, and Rita brought out coffee and her finest china cups and saucers. Don asked how they got eggs for the bannock, and Robert said they collected goose eggs. "They're real good," he added. They also occasionally went to Fort Simpson to shop for groceries because groceries in Wrigley, the nearest town, were very expensive. Don said he would send Robert some dried eggs that would keep well and could be used for his bannock. Robert gave Don his mailing address, and I gave him my e-mail address, so we could keep in contact when he was in Fort Simpson.

Phil asked Robert how to say "thank you" in the South Slavey language. "It's mahsi," he said, "pronounced *maw si.*"

We said our goodbyes at about 1:00 p.m. and said our *mashis* as well. Dan went down to the canoe and brought up venison sausage and jerky for Rita, Robert, and Victor. It's interesting how little things can bring about memorable events. If we hadn't been low on water, we would never have met them. If the wind and rain hadn't come up, our visit would have been short, and we wouldn't have learned so much about the Déné, their folklore, and how people like Robert and Rita spent their lives in the bush.

PERSEVERANCE

The water had calmed down, but as soon as we left Willowlake River, the wind picked up, and whitecaps appeared ahead of us. The wind in our faces was between 10 and 15 mph (16–24 kph). The wind was blowing south, and the river was flowing north. The whitecaps we had seen in the distance soon reached us and put us in a precarious situation. We hugged the shoreline, lowered our heads, and dug deep into the silty water. The *Ruby Ann*, my Mad River canoe, which I named for my adventurous mother, held her own. The bow lifted as it hit the front of each wave and came down with a splash on the back side of the wave. We didn't take any waves over the bow and were glad we had more weight in the back to keep the bow a little higher.

After paddling for an hour and a half, we realized we had pushed about a mile ahead of Phil and Don. It was time for a rest anyway, so we pulled onto a gravel beach and dragged our canoe safely away from the rollers that were crashing on shore. Our rest stops were much more enjoyable now that we had moved beyond the muddy shorelines we had encountered on our first few days. The river was continuing to recede from the shoreline, leaving logs to sit on and solid beaches for walking.

We continued on and then stopped once more for a short rest before River Between Two Mountains. The river is aptly named because it flows through a gap in the McConnell Mountain Range with towering peaks on either side. As we arrived at the river, we spotted a road from Highway 1 (the road to Wrigley) that came down alongside the tributary near its south bank. The gravel beach at the end of the road looked like a good spot to have dinner before we paddled on to Wrigley.

We chose to build a fire on the beach instead of in a fire ring near the tree line to avoid the mosquitoes. With the wind blowing, we could avoid the constant nuisance of the pestering little buzzing vampires. Arctic sweet peas were blooming everywhere along the flats above the riverbank, adding to the beauty of the area.

I started a fire just as Phil and Don arrived. Phil sat on his folding camp chair with a thin sheet of plywood on his lap and began cutting vegetables and sausage for our foil dinners. Our map showed the river narrowing just beyond River Between Two Mountains, and we hoped it would result in a swift current and a speedy trip to Wrigley. We would be arriving in Wrigley late in the evening, so we knew we would need to make our dinner stop as short as possible.

The afternoon and evening were uneventful, and we arrived at Wrigley at 10:30 p.m. Several boats pulled up on the shoreline were the first indication we had reached the village. A steep hillside several hundred feet high towered above the beach, and we assumed the village was on the flat above. Dan and I pulled our canoes to shore and walked up the muddy beach to a road that led to a camping area with firepits and an outhouse. We selected a suitable site about 150 ft (45.7 m) from the beach. Phil and Don arrived, and we began the challenge of carrying our gear and setting up camp. The days were getting longer as we traveled north with only a few hours of twilight each night. After the Tundra tent and our sleeping tents were erected, we unfolded our camp chairs and saluted a fine day with a shot of Yukon Jack.

It was after midnight when we retreated to our tents for the night.

38.9 mi (62.6 km) traveled today – 297.6 mi (479 km) overall

Campsite location: N63°13'30" W123°28'14.5"

ELEVEN
Johnson River

"To awaken quite alone in a strange town is one of the pleasantest sensations in the world." - Freya Stark (explorer and travel writer)

Sunday, June 25, 2006 – Wrigley to Johnson River

At 7:00 a.m. I headed over to the Tundra tent. After a while, I roused Phil, and we ate oatmeal before hiking up to Wrigley to make phone calls and buy some Coca-Cola. At home I usually drink a Coke about once every day or so. On the river we had all enjoyed that occasional shot of sugar and caffeine for a little extra energy, and now that we were finding ice along the river, an ice-cold Coke was something we relished when we could find it.

In 1965 the community of Wrigley was moved to its present site from Fort Wrigley. The high ground provided a healthier environment than the swampy location of Fort Wrigley, just downstream from River Between Two Mountains. Tuberculosis and famine had claimed the lives of more than one hundred Déné in the years before the move.

Phil and I walked up a road that paralleled the river to the north and then switched back to the south and into the village. We passed a cemetery with most of the graves surrounded by white picket fences. Two graves with flowers over mounds of fresh dirt indicated the fairly recent passing of some community members. A short distance beyond was the village.

Wrigley was designed with wide, straight streets running north/south and east/west. Elizabeth Noel wrote that they saw garbage everywhere when they stopped at Wrigley. We found just the opposite—no garbage anywhere. The town sits on a terrace high above the river. We walked down the main street, and the only person we saw was a gentleman passing us in a tanker truck. We walked to the end of town and found the co-op store, the hotel, and the mini-mart, all of which were closed.

As we turned back, we saw a gentleman walking toward us who turned out to be the driver of the tanker truck. We introduced ourselves and learned that his name was Lloyd. He told us he had gone to a clean water source and was delivering water to the homes in the village. We explained that we were paddling to Inuvik and possibly to Tuktoyaktuk on the Arctic Ocean if we could find a way to have our canoes transported back to our truck in Inuvik.

"Oh, you're the ones who stopped at Willow," he said. He had been there the day before and told us that Robert was his half-brother.

We asked him to direct us to the RCMP detachment and learned there was no longer any detachment in Wrigley. I asked if the co-op store would be opening soon. Unfortunately, since it was Sunday, we were out of luck. We told him that all we really needed was to use a phone to check in with the RCMP and call our families. He said we could go to his house and use his phone. His son Josh was there, and Lloyd said to knock on the door and tell Josh his dad said we could use the phone. He also said he had lots of soft drinks, including Coca-Cola, and we could buy a twelve-pack from him for $10.

We walked back to the house he had described, knocked on the door, and met Josh. We explained what his dad had said, and he quickly handed us the phone. We each called home and talked to our wives. Sue said she would be flying to Atlanta on July 27 with our eight-year-old grandson, Nathaniel. He lived in Georgia with his mother's family and had been out to spend the summer with his father, Reed (our son), Lisa (his stepmother), their son, Reed Evan, and their two-month-old-daughter, Caitlyn.

Our phone calls done, we said goodbye to Josh and walked back to the canoes with our Coca-Cola. When we got back to camp, I remembered we forgot to call the RCMP and check in. We tried using the satellite phone, but it wasn't working right. The man answering the phone on the other end sounded like he was speaking Chinese.

PERSEVERANCE

I walked back up to town with Don and Dan, so I could call the RCMP, and they could call home and see the village. When we arrived at Josh's house, Lloyd had returned. While Dan and Don called home, I had a nice conversation with Lloyd about the river, camp spots, and local folklore. He told us about an island just past town named Rocky Island where there was a swimming hole with warm, clear water. But he told us not to camp there because it wasn't safe. "Two kayakers camped there one night and disappeared," he said. "Their camp was intact, and their kayaks were pulled ashore, but they were gone."

By the time we had made our phone calls and returned to the river, it was almost noon. We consolidated our gear, packed our canoes, lashed down our dry bags and tubs, and left the beach by 12:30 p.m.

Twenty minutes later we stopped at Rocky Island with thoughts of a warm bath in the pool Lloyd had described. We found the pool, but the water was cold, full of silt, and a chunk of ice was nearby. We were disappointed, but it was clear that within the last few days, the river had receded below the rim of the pool, and the water didn't have enough time to become heated by the sun. In a few more days the silt would settle to the bottom, and the water temperature would rise to the level of any outdoor swimming pool back home, though it would be too late for us to enjoy.

We ate our lunch beside the pool and were on the water again by 1:15 p.m. We arrived at Ochre River two hours later. A back eddy caught our canoes just beyond the outflow, and we were able to paddle a short distance up the river. Lloyd had told us the river was clear and the water good to drink. We found the water silty until we paddled into the main flow of the stream. We paddled to a gravel beach, and Dan tried unsuccessfully to catch a fish. We pumped water until our containers were full and then bathed in the cool, clear water. It was a magical spot, so different from the silty, marshy streams we had passed over the previous eight days.

It was hard to leave that little bit of paradise, but we needed to get to the Johnson River before it got too late. We paddled out of the mouth of the Ochre River and caught the fast current of the Mackenzie. The stretch between Wrigley and Johnson River was a long, straight section with no islands.

At 7:30 p.m. we arrived at the Johnson River and found an excellent spot to camp with a fire ring on a gravel beach. After pitching our tents, we cooked baked beans, beer dogs, and mashed potatoes. We finished that off with oatmeal-raisin cookies that a man named Walter gave us at the Wrigley boat launch just before we left. Walter was a bush pilot with a contract to deliver fuel in the area. The previous night he had traveled in his boat from Norman Wells to Wrigley in six hours.

By 9:30 p.m. I was in my tent writing in my journal and then reading until I fell asleep. I reflected on that memorable day with no rain and a strong current to move us swiftly along.

37.5 mi (60.4 km) traveled today – 335.1 mi (539.4 km) overall

Campsite location: N63°42.58'30" W123°54'34"

TWELVE
Redstone River

"Today is the oldest you've ever been, and the youngest you'll ever be again." –
Eleanor Roosevelt

Monday, June 26, 2006 – Johnson River to Redstone River

What a great spot to wake up in the morning of my sixty-second birthday. There had been a small rain shower in the middle of the night. When I woke up at 5:30 a.m., I thought I heard rain again, but when I looked out at a flat white rock outside my tent, I saw no raindrops. The sound continued, and I searched to find out what was making it. That's when I realized mosquitoes between the tent and the fly were hitting the fabric in a frantic effort to get in—to get me. I hoped it was not going to be another of those days like our evening on Mills Lake.

It was warm during the night, and I hadn't needed my fleece sleeping bag liner, which I'd used for the past few days. The sun was shining at 7:45 a.m., and a stiff breeze was blowing downriver. We had talked about paddling 48 mi (77 km) to Redstone River, and with a breeze at our backs, that seemed possible.

Phil and Don left about ten minutes before Dan and me, at about 9:40 a.m. We took one last look at our camp and agreed it was one of our best. If only we could have camps like that for the rest of the trip!

By the time we began to paddle, the wind had changed direction, but there was only a slight breeze at our faces as we paddled past Dam Creek. Soon the wind picked up. I used my wind gauge to measure it and registered a steady breeze of 10 mph (16 kph) with gusts from 15 to 20 mph.

That section of the river was swifter and narrower compared to the past few days. The headwind slowed us down but not enough to force us off the river. We reached the Blackwater River which flows from Blackwater Lake, about 20 mi (32 km) east. True to its name, the water was dark in color but not as dark as some of the streams we had passed. We paddled about 1,000 ft (305 m) up the Blackwater to fish. Back in Wrigley, Lloyd had recommended that we fish the mouth of the river, so we threw in our lines for about twenty minutes before Phil and Don arrived. They had been paddling along shore much of the day while Dan and I bucked the wind farther out into the current. Fishing was not good, so we paddled out of the Blackwater and landed on a gravel bar for lunch.

I washed out a pair of socks and put them on the canoe cover to dry. Between the wind and the sun, I figured they would dry quickly.

Don did most of the food preparation for the nights that he and Phil were responsible for dinner. Don and Phil each packed their own breakfasts and lunches, as did Dan and I. With Don's backpacker mindset, he seemed to be running out of food. From our experience on the Yukon, the three of us had learned how exhausting it was to paddle all day, unload the gear, carry it to the campsite, set up the tents, cook dinner, take everything down in the morning, pack it up, carry it down to the shore, and load and secure the gear in the canoes. All that took a lot of energy and required more food than we would normally eat. Don's hikes were usually for just a few days where fewer calories wasn't a problem. Dan and I packed on the heavy side, believing it would be better to have too much food than not enough. In addition, canoes can carry many times more gear and supplies than a backpack. Don was running short of food for his lunches, and we knew we would soon be sharing some of our surplus until we reached Norman Wells and retrieved the boxes of supplies we had shipped from Hay River.

As we paddled along, we admired the abundance of gravel and sandy beaches showing as a result of the receding water level. There were so many excellent options for campsites. We had passed a fishing camp before Blackwater River, and we expected to see more of them. It was hard to distinguish day from night because the sun was up almost twenty-four hours a day. Even when the sun set on the horizon for a couple of hours, it was light enough to read all night. When I lived in Fairbanks, AK, and was working twelve hours a day fueling airplanes at the Fairbanks International Airport during the summer, I would often start fishing the Chena River at 11:00 p.m. On the longest day of the year, the

Fairbanks collegiate summer baseball team, the Alaska Goldpanners, play their annual Midnight Sun Game, which starts at 10:30 p.m. and concludes around 1:30 a.m. with no artificial lighting.

Don brought a new tent for our trip, and in the campgrounds on the way to Fort Providence, he had some difficulty putting it up. Dan gave him a hand, and since there was plenty of room inside, they decided to share the tent to save space. Dan left his small pup tent in the truck. When one went to bed before the other, he would joke, "I'll keep the light on for ya," mocking the Motel 6 advertisements.

Phil and I were having sharp stabbing pains in the back of our necks each day after an hour or so of paddling. I had experienced similar pains on the Yukon trip in 2001. I would move my head around and rub my neck, but it didn't help. Dan was having a little soreness in his back. These were irritants to all three of us but nothing that would keep us from reaching our goal. We would just "suck it up" and carry on.

We were constantly thinking about water for drinking and cooking. We were conserving water because there wasn't an abundance of clean water anywhere along the Mackenzie. We also had to be sure not to become dehydrated. This became a balancing act, and when we found an ample supply of clean water, we hydrated our bodies and filled our containers to the brim. Before we left the Blackwater, we collected enough water to get us through the next two days.

At times I found myself longing to be finished with the trip, but I never considered giving up. I didn't feel that way very often because every day brought something new and exciting. The people we met along the river, the scenery, the food, and the camaraderie made it such a superb trip.

We left the Blackwater at 2:10 p.m. The wind was hitting us hard in the face. The Mackenzie wound to the left and then to the right. The current was moving fast, which made the wind seem stronger and the waves bigger. Along the left bank was a burn area that extended over 60 mi (97 km). We had paddled quite a bit ahead of Phil and Don, and with the swift water and wind, we wanted to stay closer. We pulled over to a rocky beach and waited. When they arrived, we continued on. Forty-five minutes later, Phil said he was ready for a break. He suggested we check out an island just ahead, and if there was a good spot, we should stop and fix dinner. With the speed of the river and the close proximity of the island, we needed to turn on the power and dig deep and fast, or we would be pushed past it before we got to shore.

We found a respectable beach and arrived at 4:30 p.m. With the river flowing rapidly along the edge of the beach, landing was a challenge. I spotted some ice on the south end of the island, and once our canoes were secure, I hiked over and found a chunk of ice more than 3 ft (0.9 m) thick. I used my Leatherman multi-tool to chip off some small pieces and put them in my collapsible bucket. The ice was covered with pebbles, sand, and dirt, so I took it down to the river and washed it clean. When the debris was gone, I had several crystal-clear pieces of ice, as clear as the ice sculptures you see at fancy events. Instead of cooling the cans of Coca-Cola, as we had done before, we were able to put the clean, clear ice crystals in our cups with the Coke.

I built a fire with twigs and small branches from along the high water mark. Dan sawed sections off a dry log that would make excellent coals and added them to the fire. Phil and Don began cutting up vegetables, and Dan scraped some mold off his venison sausage and cut it into small squares. By then we were all expert foil dinner chefs.

Phil and Don were both seventy years old at the time of that trip. Neither looked their age, and watching them paddle, you would think they were much younger. They had a hard time keeping up with us, but that was primarily because I had a "mountain man" in the front of my canoe. Dan was muscular, very strong, determined, and younger that the rest of us. Dan and I were both impressed with Phil and Don and hoped we would be able to paddle like them when we were seventy.

After dinner, Dan and I each ate three of our Sun Maid Oatmeal cookies, sitting in our chairs relaxing and appreciating Walter's donation to our trip. Phil and Don had finished theirs the day before. The wind had quit completely by that time, and at 6:40 p.m., it was very hot. It had been in the 80s Fahrenheit (mid to high 20s Celsius) during the day, and it hadn't come down much in the evening. With the wind blowing, the heat wasn't bad. But with no breeze that evening, it wasn't pleasant.

By 7:00 p.m. we were on the water again. A seagull was flying circles above Phil and Don, complaining about something, but then it settled down on the water. We passed on the left side of Birch Island and noticed the fire had apparently jumped across the river at that point because all the trees were black, dead, and falling.

When we reached Redstone River, the beach to the south of the river was muddy and not conducive to camping. We crossed the mouth of the river and scraped the bottom of the canoe several times. After passing the Redstone, we found a possible campsite on a large gravel bar. Most of the bar was covered with damp mud and had apparently been under water only a few days before. Higher up the beach, near the bank, we found a dry, sandy spot to pitch our tents.

Don fixed pudding for all of us in celebration of my birthday. By 10:30 p.m. I was in my hot tent reading. The sun was still shining brightly, and I could read without my headlamp at 11:30 p.m.

48.3 mi (77.7 km) traveled – 383.4 mi (617.1 km) overall

Campsite location: N64°17'31" W124°33'35"

THIRTEEN
South of Seagull Island

"A day without laughter is a day wasted." – Charlie Chaplin

Tuesday, June 27, 2006 – Redstone River to an Island Just South of Seagull Island

After waking and reading for half an hour, I unzipped my tent and looked for the nearest bush to relieve myself. I was usually the first up in the morning, and Phil teased me about my morning sound—the tent being unzipped. Apparently, that sound got the others moving because they were soon up, rolling up their sleeping bags and preparing coffee. Not being a coffee drinker, I didn't partake in that morning ritual. I had slept well, and it was a pleasant morning. Clouds had formed above, and dark clouds were billowing to the east with the potential of rain if they moved our way. The sky was clear to the north though, so we were banking on good weather.

The river was dropping more each day. Our canoes were close to the river when we went to bed, but in the morning they were 10 ft (3 m) from the water. Everyone moved quickly, anxious to be on the river. After eating breakfast and packing up, we left the riverbank at about 8:45 a.m. The river was very fast as we paddled past Keel River, also known as Gravel River.

In August 1896 a prospector named George Carmack—along with his Tagish wife, Kate, and her brother, Skookum Jim, plus a nephew, Dawson Charlie—discovered gold on Bonanza Creek, a tributary of the Klondike River in the Yukon. After staking their claims, they traveled downriver to file the claims at the police post at the mouth of Fortymile River. Many prospectors were in the region at the time, and when they heard of the find, they stampeded to the Klondike to stake their own claims. My great-grandfather, Noah Davey, was among them. He filed a claim on Magnet Gulch, close to the discovery claim. His discovery was chronicled in the cleanup edition of the Dawson City newspaper.

When word spread that the Klondike was one of the richest gold fields ever discovered, people from all over the world rushed to the area, hoping to arrive before all the claims were taken. Most of the stampeders traveled by boat from Seattle, Portland, or San Francisco, landing in Alaska at Dyea or Skagway and then packing their gear over either Chilkoot Pass or White Pass. Most spent the winter at Bennet Lake where they constructed boats and rafts that would take them down the Yukon River to the gold fields.

Many attempted to reach the Klondike via other routes, most of which were extremely difficult or disastrous. Businessmen in Seattle, Portland, San Francisco, and Skagway were making fortunes selling mining supplies to the stampeders, and several unscrupulous businessmen in Edmonton created their own opportunity. They spread word that there was an eastern route to the gold fields from Edmonton, down the Mackenzie River and over the mountains. James A. Michener, in his novel Journey, tells a story about some of those adventurers who attempted to reach the gold fields from the east. His fictitious group spent a winter where the Keel River empties into the Mackenzie, waiting for the snow and ice to melt before continuing on.

We passed Saline Island, and after a few twists and turns, we stopped at a little island not far west of Mio Lake. A power boat passed us, an indication we were getting close to civilization. The clouds were building, and it looked like there would be showers sometime that day. It was cool and comfortable paddling into the wind. We had already traveled 17 mi (27 km) by the time we stopped.

After our half-hour break, we continued on, traveling some 8.5 mi (13.5 km) per hour. We passed Dry Island on our left and then three more islands heading toward Old Fort Point. Large chunks of ice lined the shore for more than a mile. We hoped to have lunch near the point but couldn't find a suitable beach. We looked at a small gravel spot but decided to find a better one. Unfortunately, the terrain got worse. A flock of more than one hundred ducks rose up from the small bushes growing out of the high water along the shoreline

We paddled beyond the point, continuing to look for a suitable spot for lunch. The river bent to the left around a 3-mile-long (5-km) island. Looking through his field glasses, Dan spotted a gravel beach at the upriver end of the island. It was a tricky maneuver to reach the beach because the river was moving swiftly on both sides of the island. We were able to land successfully, but the current caught Phil and Don's canoe, and they landed far down the beach from us. They grabbed their painters and lined their canoe up to us.

We spent an hour on the island, eating and resting. I watched Don sitting quietly as the rest of us began slicing cheese and sausage for our crackers, pulling nuts from our dry bags, and beginning to eat. He was out of food for his lunches and was too polite and perhaps too embarrassed to ask us to share ours. We had offered him food the day before, but he had declined. I knew he was hungry, and I decided it was time to make another offer. Don was an avowed Republican among three Democrats, and over the past fifteen days, we had good-naturedly engaged in several political discussions. In keeping with that, I turned to him and asked if he would like some crackers and cheese.

"Sure! That would be nice," he said.

"Say, 'I love Bill Clinton,'" I replied. Aside from being a Republican, Don has a superb sense of humor.

"I love Bill Clinton," he said, giggling. We all had a good laugh, with Don laughing the loudest.

By 3:10 p.m. we had finished lunch and were back on the water, heading toward Seagull Island. After having such a difficult time finding a landing for lunch, we were concerned about finding a location to camp for the night. We paddled close to the shore of a small island, watching for a suitable site and thinking it might be better to make an early camp rather than spend hours looking later. We spotted a nice beach, and I climbed out of the canoe to inspect the shoreline. After walking away from the water and along the shore, I declared it to be the perfect spot. Just as we started to pitch our tents, the wind began to howl, and rain began to fall.

Every night so far, we had put the Tundra tent up in the same configuration with each corner the same height and the center pole higher yet. If we pitched the tent in a similar fashion there, the strong gusts would turn it into a kite. Instead, we assembled it with one edge of the nylon top touching the ground. We placed heavy rocks on the nylon to keep it down and put up two corner poles at their regular height and the center pole half that height. Our theory was that the wind would blow up and over the tent, as long as the wind continued

PERSEVERANCE

in the same direction. The lean-to design looked good, so we hunkered down under the Tundra tent, and Don cooked bannock on the camp stove.

When the rain let up, we built a fire and sat around it while Don cooked one of his gourmet delights, "corn shrimp bake." When it was ready, we dug in and opened a couple of cans of Coca-Cola to share.

The river continued to drop. Since landing, 3 ft (0.9 m) of space had been exposed between the river and the canoes. I saw blue sky to the south at 8:40 p.m. when I crawled into my tent for the night. We were almost 30 mi (48 km) ahead of where we expected to be by that date. Over dinner, we had decided to be back on the river by 8:00 a.m., so I set my alarm for 7:00 a.m.

42.2 mi (67.9 km) traveled today – 425.6 mi (685 km) overall

Campsite location: N64°42'39.8" W125°05'38.3"

The four of us in Washington State, ready to depart

Riverboat Noweta docked on Great Slave Lake in Hay River

Canoes loaded and ready for departure from Fort Providence

PERSEVERANCE

Rest stop in high water on Mills Lake

First campsite along Mills Lake

Northern Pike caught by John in a slough along Mills Lake

PERSEVERANCE

Foil dinners cooking on the shore of Mills Lake

Clean, clear ice taken from one of the massive blocks along the river

Cabins at Brownings Landing

Dan with Angus Sanchez at Jean Marie River

PERSEVERANCE

Dan, Don and John in front of ice left from breakup

Wrigley ferry crossing

Early morning departure

Phil ready to zap mosquitos in the Tundra tent

PERSEVERANCE

Robert Hardisty sharing stories by the fire in his teepee

Robert showing us furs he trapped during the winter

Robert's uncle Victor Pauncha-Boot

Robert and Rita at Xahndah (Willowlake River)

PERSEVERANCE

Robert getting bannock ready for the fry pan

Church of the Holy Heart of Mary in Wrigley

Lunch and a snooze after a long morning of paddling

Phil and Don paddling their Mad River canoe

PERSEVERANCE

Phil cutting vegetables for foil dinners

Tundra tent pitched to handle strong winds

FOURTEEN
Halfway Island

"Only where children gather is there any real chance of fun." — Mignon McLaughlin, (journalist and author)

Wednesday, June 28, 2006 – From Just South of Seagull Island to Halfway Island

I woke to the sound of a tent being unzipped, zipped again, unzipped, and zipped again. "It's seven o'clock!" Dan shouted. That was the time we had agreed we would get up, but my watch said 6:00 a.m.

"No, it's not!" I yelled back. "It's only six!"

"Not in Mountain Time!" Dan replied. It was a bit of a surprise that we had entered a different time zone. None of us except Dan had changed our watches from Pacific Time to Mountain Time.

I started rolling my sleeping bag and Thermarest and then decided to set my watch to the correct time later. We were all quickly out of our tents and eating breakfast when Don told us to look at our canoes. The river had dropped at least a foot overnight and our canoes were several feet farther from the river than they were when we went to bed.

The Tundra tent configuration worked well, protecting us from the wind and rain during dinner and again in the morning as we ate breakfast. We broke camp and were on the river by 8:15 a.m. Phil and Don left ten minutes before us, but it wasn't long until we passed them. Soon afterward a stiff wind kicked up, and we fought it until we got to Police Island. We found a gravel beach with several large chunks of ice the size of cargo containers.

A half-hour rest recharged our bodies, and then we got into our canoes once again. The river became narrower as it wound around Police Island and turned west. After a few minutes of paddling, Dan and I crossed at an angle to the north bank to be on the same side of the river as Tulita (Fort Norman), some 14 mi (23 km) downriver. The wind was blowing from the west and began to increase in intensity, hitting us broadside as we reached the middle of the river. I questioned my judgement of crossing, because the swells struck the side of the canoe and water sprayed over the gunwales. Turning around in the middle of that fury was out of the question, so we dug in, maintained our speed, and twenty minutes later made it to the north shore. Stretching above the beach were fifty-foot cliffs of exposed gravel, sand, clay, and what looked like seams of coal. Phil and Don were getting closer. They had crossed directly from the island and avoided the strongest wind.

We paddled slowly, watching ravens perched in the trees at the top of the bank. Swallows played in the wind, dipping and making abrupt turns as they pursued the few insects braving the wind. Phil and Don closed the gap, and we paddled together until we reached a black sand beach about 40 ft (12.2 m) long, a good spot for lunch. I estimated that we were about one half hour from Tulita.

Once we were back on the water and had paddled for about fifteen minutes, we rounded a point and saw the boat launch at Tulita. Previously named Fort Norman, the hamlet of almost 500 residents was renamed Tulita (Where the Waters Meet) in 1996. Above the launch, several buildings were visible, and three young boys gave us directions to the store. They said to paddle to the white sign and walk up the road to the Northern Store.

Don stayed with the canoes as Dan, Phil and I walked into the town. Fresh food is a prized commodity for river travelers as well as residents of small villages along the river. At the store a bundle of carrots sold for $4.00, and a head of lettuce sold for $4.89. Our other prized commodity was Coca-Cola, which sold for $18.00 for a twelve-pack. I wondered how the town's inhabitants and those living in the surrounding area could afford such prices. Since we had run out of fresh vegetables, we were happy to pay the prevailing prices, so we could have more foil dinners.

Tulita's streets were not paved, and the parking lot in front of the store was so rutted that customers parked along the street rather than risk their vehicles.

The store was located at the corner of an intersection. Across the street was a post office, an arena, and what looked like the band headquarters. Down the street toward the river on a knoll was an old square building that I assumed was part of the fort of Fort Norman. When I asked, a Déné man named Jimmy explained it was the old Hudson's Bay store.

I found a telephone and called the local RCMP but didn't get an answer. Then I called Jack Kruger at the number he had provided and explained our location and that I wasn't able to check in with the RCMP. The connection with Jack was intermittent, but enough of the information seemed to be heard as Jack thanked me for the call. I wasn't going to pass up an opportunity to call home and was fortunate to connect right away with Sue.

As we walked back toward the canoes, a young Caucasian man in shorts, a Nike T-shirt, and hiking boots struck up a conversation and asked Phil if we were traveling the river. We affirmed that we were, and he introduced himself as Mike Jordan, the RCMP officer assigned to Tulita. It was his day off, but he had seen us and asked if we had reported in yet. I explained that we had contacted Jack Kruger because we didn't get an answer when we called the RCMP.

Mike was completing a two-year assignment in Tulita, and his wife was a nurse, working at the local health center. He would be leaving on July 10 for his next assignment in a town in British Columbia, just across the border from Danville, WA, and not far from where Dan was building a cabin and would eventually be living. He told us about the difficulties of living and working in Tulita, where there was a great deal of substance abuse. "The elders, those who have the culture of the past, are getting too old to pass it on," he said. "The younger ones don't care about learning the culture, and there isn't much to do, so they get into trouble. There has been a huge oil discovery, and there will be lots of money for the band. I'm worried about how this might affect the people here."

He told us that while he was stationed at Fort McPherson, an elder told him that the white man bringing alcohol was not the reason for the abuse. The elder said that for centuries they had made and drank a brew, but in moderation. However, alcohol and drugs were more plentiful now. Mike understood that the problem was more complex than just one cause. He told us that if they didn't come up with an answer soon, their culture will be destroyed.

PERSEVERANCE

It was clear to me that Mike had a deep concern for the people of Tulita. I hoped the person who took his place would have the same interest and concern. It takes time to build a relationship in any new community, but when the community is caught between the old ways of the elders and the new ways embraced by the young, building relationships is an even greater challenge. The bond that Mike created couldn't just be passed on to his replacement but would need to be built from scratch. Two-year cycles aren't conducive to building a long-term bond between the RCMP and the people of Tulita. Perhaps one answer to this dilemma would be to find a young, capable member of the community to be trained as a RCMP officer who could be stationed in Tulita on a permanent basis.

As Mike walked down to the river with us, he said he didn't have much time to fish and enjoy the area. He would need to come back on vacation to enjoy it.

The three young boys we spoke to as we arrived in Tulita came to chat and see us off. They asked where we were going, and we told them, "To Inuvik and maybe Tuk (Tuktoyaktuk)."

"My grandparents live in Tuk," one boy said. "The purple house." With constant smiles on their faces, they asked us questions about our canoes and gear. Mike stood by with a grin on his face as he watched the happy young boys. They all said goodbye, and a young woman on the shoreline advised us to stay out of the middle of the river as we pulled our canoes off the muddy beach and into the water.

Just past Tulita we saw the clear waters of the Great Bear River, the outflow of Great Bear Lake, the eighth-largest lake in the world. On the far side of the outlet, we pulled into the outflow to pump silt-free water into our containers.

Deline, a small town on the western shore of Great Bear Lake, was the winter quarters of Sir John Franklin's famed second expedition from 1825 to 1827 when he floated down the Great Bear River to the Mackenzie River and then down to the Arctic Ocean and west along its shoreline. The village was known as Fort Franklin until 1993 when the official name became Deline which means "Where the Waters Flow."

We pushed on down the river and looked up to see three rockslides on the side of Bear Rock. Each slide was in the oval shape of a beaver pelt. Robert Hardisty told us we would see the giant beaver pelts on the side of a mountain, and he was correct.

Five miles (8 km) downriver, we passed an empty barge pushed by a tugboat on its way upriver. It threw out a sizeable wake, but we headed into the swell and passed through it safely. The wind continued but died down enough that it didn't hamper our paddling. After a short break and more paddling, we began looking for a campsite at around 8:00 p.m. We located a suitable beach at the upriver end of Halfway Island. The beach was relatively level but muddy and extended a long distance from the island itself. It was apparent that most of the beach had recently been under water. Up closer to the island was a dry gravel area where we pitched our tents and prepared for dinner. Dan cooked up chicken fettucine Alfredo while Don made bannock. As we ate dinner at 9:45 p.m., a beautiful rainbow appeared in the east.

As I lay in my sleeping bag on my Thermarest air mattress, away from the mosquitoes, I thought about the events of the day. Although there were many memorable events, the highlight was talking to Sue and learning that the family was doing well.

44.2 mi (71.1 km) traveled today – 469.8 mi (756.1 km) overall

Campsite location: N64°59'09.3" W125°06'56.9"

FIFTEEN
One Mile South of Prohibition Creek

"Adopt the pace of nature: her secret is patience." – Ralph Waldo Emerson

Thursday, June 29, 2006 – Halfway Island to One Mile South of Prohibition Creek

The sun was shining on my tent when I woke up at 5:15 a.m. I noticed our days on the river often began with sunshine, and then clouds would develop on the horizon and eventually moved over the river. Everyone was up and eating breakfast by 7:00 a.m. As we broke camp, clouds began to form, but there was no wind. I expected the wind would come up on our way to Norman Wells, which was just beyond the halfway point of our expedition.

Halfway Island is actually three islands separated by narrow sloughs. Our camp was on the southwest shore of the first island, which was where we shoved off at 8:45 a.m. The current took us out into the main flow, and we quickly passed the other two islands. Once we passed the last island, the wind arrived, whitecaps formed on the top of each wave, and a sprinkle of rain began to fall. After an hour of pounding from the wind and waves, we worked our way over to the northeast shore, hoping to find calmer water.

The sprinkle was subsiding as Dan and I pulled ashore. We waited a few minutes for Phil and Don to catch up, and then we all continued downriver, keeping close to the safety of the shoreline. Mike Jordan had told us the previous day that the strong headwinds were not typical for that time of year, and there had been more rain than usual. We were ready for a change to cooler temperatures, a break from the 85°F (29.5°C) weather we had experienced almost every day thus far. We were well prepared for such weather, but we preferred clear skies and a gentle breeze at our backs.

By 11:15 a.m. the wind increased considerably, and the bows of our canoes were being lifted and pounded down into the next wave. A severe storm was developing downriver and coming our way. I was working hard to keep the canoe faced into the waves, and Dan was trying to keep his paddle in the water as the bow of the canoe was lifted up on each wave. Dan and I had to shout at each other to be heard over the roar of the wind and waves. We knew we needed to get to shore, but we also knew we couldn't allow the waves to hit us broadside. We headed for shore at an angle downriver, moving steadily forward to keep the waves from filling the canoe with water. The spray skirt kept most of the water out, something for which we were most grateful.

We landed on a small beach but struggled to get out of the canoe as waves crashed ashore, each one hitting the side of the canoe and rocking it violently from side to side. Once we were out, we pulled the canoe safely away from the waves and then sat down on the gravel to catch our breath.

Phil and Don were within sight but at least half a mile behind. When they arrived, we steadied their canoe so they could climb out and helped them pull it to safety. We sat on the beach, watching the waves pound the shoreline. Several seagulls seemed to be enjoying the wind, swooping and catching gusts that took them high above the beach. By early afternoon the wind had not decreased, so we sat and waited. None of us were interested in being on the river in such conditions.

I decided to measure the wind velocity using a compact anemometer I had purchased in the spring and found sustained winds of 20 mph (32 kph) and gusts up above 30 mph. The wind was blowing up the river, and the rolling waves had several miles to build. A sprinkle of rain started, and I grabbed my red nylon tarp. A large log lay parallel to the shore about 10 ft (3 m) from the river. Another log lay somewhat perpendicular across the large log, so we collected an assortment of poles and other driftwood to build a lean-to that would support the tarp. After clearing out the sticks and other debris that had collected next to the log, we leveled the gravel and had a fine shelter to protect us from the wind and rain. We could see the storm had no immediate plans of dying down, so we made ourselves comfortable.

PERSEVERANCE

Late in the afternoon, a floatplane circled above us three times. At one point it appeared the plane would land on the river in front of us. At the end of the third round, it landed near the outflow of Prohibition Creek, about a mile downriver. From our location we couldn't see the plane once it landed, but we were curious what it might be doing there. We were also concerned about the safety of the plane and its passengers, landing and taking off from the river in such harsh conditions. Two hours later the plane left and seemed to have no trouble getting airborne.

During a break in the rain, I started a fire, and we roasted some of Dan's venison pepperoni. Later, Don cooked spaghetti.

The wind continued without any sign of letting up. At 7:00 p.m., we decided to spend the night. Phil and I each found suitable locations for our tents, but Dan and Don decided to spend the night in the lean-to. A positive result of the wind was the absence of mosquitoes. Phil turned on the satellite phone at 8:00 p.m., something he promised his wife, Kathy, he would do each night. At that point, I headed for my tent, read for a few minutes, and then went to sleep.

13 mi (20.9 km) traveled today – 482.8 mi (777 km) overall

Campsite location: N65°07'55.5" W126°16'07.3"

SIXTEEN
Norman Wells

"The danger of adventure is worth a thousand days of ease and comfort." – Paulo Coelho (Brazilian lyricist and novelist)

Friday, June 30, 2006 – One Mile South of Prohibition Creek to Norman Wells

At 8:00 a.m. I realized I had been in my tent for almost twelve hours—reading, sleeping, and waiting out the storm. The waves continued to crash on shore. The wind seemed to have died down some, but the river was still a dangerous place for a canoe. It was obvious we should continue waiting.

I left my tent and checked on Dan and Don. They were sleeping peacefully under the lean-to. I walked over to Phil's tent and looked through the plastic window of his rain fly and saw that he, too, was asleep.

I walked down to the canoe and emptied water that had collected in small pools on the spray cover. I dug into one of my dry bags, located a new book, since I had just finished one, and went back to my tent to read and wait out the storm. An hour later, Phil came by to check on me, so I got up. Dan and Don were just rousing themselves from the lean-to, and we all gathered to assess our situation.

The sky was beginning to clear. There were still whitecaps on the river, but the waves breaking on shore were smaller. We were all anxious to get back on the river but were not willing to take extensive risks just to reach Norman Wells by the end of the day. Weighing all the risks and benefits, we decided to pack

PERSEVERANCE

up and paddle close to shore until we reached a point near Prohibition Creek and then review our options. A major consideration was getting to the office of the Northern Transportation Company Ltd. before it closed at 4:00 p.m. to pick up the boxes of supplies we had shipped from Hay River. If we didn't make it in time, we would have to stay in Norman Wells until the office opened on Tuesday, following the Canada Day weekend. We concluded that we should be able to make it with time to spare as long as we left soon. The one factor we couldn't control was the wind.

We heated water for coffee and instant oatmeal, ate our breakfast, and then quickly packed up. By 11:00 a.m. we were on the river. The water was choppy, but we made good headway.

When we reached the point near Prohibition Creek, we saw several yellow canoes and lots of young Déné boys on the beach. It was apparent the floatplane we had seen the day before had made contact with that group for some reason.

Fighting the wind and waves slowed our progress, and we concluded that if we kept our speed down to stay with Phil and Don, our arrival before 4:00 p.m. in Norman Wells was questionable. Dan and I told Phil and Don that we were going to dig in and try to make it to town in time. We encouraged them to take their time and be safe.

As we rounded the point, we were confronted with strong headwinds. The water became rougher and occasionally washed over the gunwales. Several times I had to bail water to keep us afloat. My arm muscles were burning with pain, but I continued to dig deep and twist the paddle on each stroke to keep the canoe straight. The sharp pain at the back of my neck began again and was aggravated with each pull of the paddle. When I told Dan that I needed a rest, he shouted, "Yes!"

We stopped at a point of land for ten minutes to have some nuts, chocolate, and water. We hadn't been able to drink water on the river because if we stopped paddling, we could get pushed into a position where a wave could hit us broadside and potentially capsize us.

After passing several small points of land, we began seeing cabins—a sure sign that we were getting close to civilization. We paddled close to shore where two young boys were riding a four-wheeler and asked them where the town was. They said to go to the second dock.

We paddled on, looking for two docks. After some time we saw what appeared to be a manmade narrow point of land stretching out into the river, which we assumed was the first dock. At the end were steel plates driven into the mud to protect the gravel and rock from the river. We paddled to the upriver side of the point, secured the canoe, climbed over large rocks, and looked for someone who could tell us if NTCL was at that location or farther downriver. A young man driving a pickup truck stopped when we flagged him down. He said he had just arrived in town the previous day and didn't know where anything was. A few moments later, a young Déné man driving a road grader came by, and we asked him where we could find NTCL. He said the office was at the second dock. We couldn't see a second dock, but he pointed downriver and said it would probably take us an hour to paddle there. I looked at my watch and saw that it was five minutes until 3:00 p.m. I explained that if we hurried, we had just enough time to get there on time.

"No, you don't," the young man said. "They close in five minutes, at four o'clock." I realized I had forgotten to change my watch from Pacific Time to Mountain Time, even though Dan had told me of the change a few days before. "I'll call Georgie," the young man said. I didn't know who Georgie was, but I assumed it was someone who worked for NTCL. He pulled out his cell phone, spoke for a few minutes, and then said Georgie would wait for us. We thanked him and then ran back to the canoe.

It took most of an hour to reach the second dock. My arm muscles were burning as the bow scraped on the gravel beach. I climbed out, quickly removed my life jacket, and threw it in the canoe. I didn't think I had time to change from my rubber boots to my New Balance camp shoes, so I kept them on. I ran up the road leading away from the dock and found the office two blocks later. The front door was unlocked, so I walked in. Georgie didn't appear to be in a hurry. She was sitting at a desk and gave me a very warm welcome. She had me sign for our provisions and helped me carry them out. Once we were outside, she asked where I would be taking them. When I told her that we were setting up a camp on the beach, she said, "Let's put them in my truck, and I'll drive you down there."

In the truck, Georgie asked if this was my first time to Norman Wells. I indicated it was, so she offered to drive me around to see the town. I asked if there was a laundromat and a place to take showers. "No laundromat," she said, "and no place with public showers." However, she took me past a motel where she said they would probably allow us to wash our clothes and take showers. In

PERSEVERANCE

front of the hotel, a young man was setting up a gas barbecue, and Georgie told me that at 7:00 p.m. he would be grilling hamburgers and hot dogs to sell.

Georgie also told me about the town's Canada Day celebrations scheduled for the next two days, including a free pancake breakfast and a free barbecue at noon. She also pointed out the liquor store and said if we wanted beer or liquor, we needed to be there before 8:00 p.m. because it would be closed for the next three days. When Georgie took me to the shore and helped me unload our boxes of provisions, I invited her to stop by that night for a beer. She said she thought she would.

Don and Phil arrived at 6:00 p.m. Don watched the canoes as Dan, Phil, and I walked into town. We stopped by the liquor store first to see if they sold Styrofoam ice chests. They told us they were sold out and suggested we try the Northern Store. The line at the liquor store was already long as the locals stocked up for the weekend celebration. We walked over to the hotel Georgie had recommended and spoke to Terry, who was not only grilling hamburgers and hot dogs but also ribs and steaks to sell along with salad. We ordered four hamburgers, and Terry said he would let us know when they were ready if we wanted to stop in the bar to have a beer. I went into the hotel but found no one to ask about showers and washing our clothes, so I joined Phil and Dan in the bar.

I told the bartender I'd like to speak to someone in the hotel about showers and laundry. She dialed someone on her phone and when she didn't get an answer asked me to follow her outside. We walked up to Terry, and she explained what we wanted.

"Oh, you're the guys paddling," Terry said. "We're all set up to let you take showers and wash your clothes." Georgie had called the owner's wife, she had called her husband, Larry, and Larry had called Terry. The news of our arrival was spreading quickly. "Stop by any time tomorrow," Terry said. "Larry will be at the hotel all day."

We quickly ate our hamburgers, stopped at the Northern Store to buy a Styrofoam ice chest, and then went to the bar for ice. The bartender gave us a big bag of ice at no charge. Then we went back to the liquor store for beer. I found a phone and called Sue while Dan and Phil bought the beer. I learned that Sue had been rear ended at a stoplight and was having to deal with that situation. Otherwise, things were going well at home.

We walked back to the beach and gave Don his hamburger. Then we set up our chairs and popped open our beers. It was our first opportunity for rest since we left the beach that morning. While we were relaxing, Mike Mitchell, a teacher from Hay River, dropped by to meet us. He explained that he was one of the leaders of the boys in yellow canoes who we had passed in the morning. They were paddling from Wrigley, carrying the Canada Games Torch in a relay across Canada. The torch had been in Nunavut previously and would be in the Yukon next. He and the other adults in his entourage were members of the Northwest Territories Parks and Recreation Association. He said that if we paddled to Tuktoyaktuk, he would pick up our canoes for us at the NTCL office if we shipped them to Hay River. In addition, he said he would make arrangements to have them shipped to us in the States. It seemed that everyone we had met so far on the river was friendly, generous, and anxious to help. We thanked Mike and explained that our truck was waiting for us in Inuvik, and we hoped to get the canoes shipped from Tuk to Inuvik if we paddled that far.

The evening was warm, the wind had died down, and we heard people in homes on the flat area above the riverbank getting started with their Canada Day celebrations. It was good to hear the laughter of lots of people having a good time after so many quiet nights on the river. We hoped Georgie would come down to join us for a beer, but as it began to get dark, we decided she likely had other things to do.

As we sat under the Tundra tent, each having a second beer, a young man stopped by and offered us an invitation from Georgie to walk up to her home for a beer. Dan offered to watch the canoes and our gear, and Phil, Don, and I followed the young man up the steep bank to Georgie's home, which overlooked the river.

A large group had gathered there, and it was apparent that was the site of most of the celebrating we had heard from the beach. On a deck facing the river, a group of about twenty people welcomed us, offered us beer, and asked about our trip. It was a diverse group of friendly folks who had lots of advice. A Déné woman, Lisa McDonald, said she had seen us in Tulita, and she was the one who gave us advice to stay out of the middle of the river.

We had a wonderful time learning from each person and sharing experiences. Georgie gifted us with a book titled *The Sahtu Atlas, Maps and Stories from the Sahtu Settlement Area in Canada's Northwest Territories*. The Sahtu Settlement Area includes large portions along the Mackenzie River, including Tulita, Norman Wells, and Fort Good Hope. It also encompasses the area surrounding Great Bear Lake. The book tells of the history of the region, the people, the physical elements, wildlife, resources, and development. It was clear to us that this was a very special gift, one we hoped we deserved. Each of our new friends wrote encouraging messages in the atlas and signed their names to one of the back pages.

By midnight we were about ready to leave when Don said that Lisa McDonald and her husband had invited us to their home across the street. Lisa and Don had had a conversation about moose hunting in which Don mentioned he had never tasted moose meat. We walked over to their home, and Lisa cooked each of us a moose steak. Before we left, she gave Don a book and me a hammer that had been left on the Canol Trail. As we were leaving the MacDonalds' home, Lisa encouraged us to stop and visit her Uncle Wilfred who lived alone along the river near Oscar Creek

The Canol Trail runs along a road that was built from Norman Wells to the Yukon Territory during World War II. The road was used in the construction of a four-inch-wide pipeline to transfer light crude Norman Wells oil to a refinery in Whitehorse. This project was overseen by the United States government in an effort to bring the oil to Alaska to support the war effort. The pipeline was used for only fourteen months and then shut down and abandoned in 1945. Another pipeline was constructed in the early 1980s for oil to be pumped from Norman Wells to Zama, Alberta.

In August 2016 we paddled the Big Salmon River in the Yukon Territories. Don was unable to make the trip because his wife was ill, but Dan paddled with me, and a friend, Ron Abo, paddled with Phil. We hired an outfitter to transport us to Quiet Lake where we began our ten-day paddle down the Big Salmon and into the Yukon River, finishing at Carmacks. Part of the trip to Quiet Lake was along a section of the Canol Pipeline. Sections of the four-inch pipe were still lying along the old road.

14.9 mi (24.0 km) traveled today – 497.7 mi (801 km) overall

Campsite location: N65°16'44.3" W126°50'06.95"

SEVENTEEN
Canada Day

"There are no limits to the majestic future which lies before the mighty expanse of Canada with its virile, aspiring, cultured, and generous-hearted people." –
Winston Churchill

Saturday, July 1, 2006 – A Day of Rest and Celebration in Norman Wells

Before I went to bed, I reset my watch to Mountain time. The air was still and warm—a big difference from earlier in the day. It took me a long time to get to sleep.

I woke up around 7:30 a.m. with the sound of wind flapping the fabric of my tent fly. I gathered all my dirty clothes and headed for the hotel. Larry, the owner, was working in the coffee shop. I introduced myself, and he told me he had a room ready for us to shower. It was one of his hotel rooms, which was under renovation. Since we didn't need to sleep there, an empty room was ideal for us to shower and change. A few feet down the hall from the room was a laundry room for his hotel staff. He charged us only $50 for the room and the use of the machines. He even provided soap and shampoo for the shower and detergent for the washer. I put a load of clothes in the washer and took a quick shower, which felt magnificent. I used the phone in the room to call the RCMP. The man who answered was in Yellowknife but said he would let the local RCMP know we had arrived in Norman Wells.

PERSEVERANCE

I walked back down to our camp, and then Dan, Don, and I walked back up to the hotel while Phil kept watch over our gear. Dan took a shower while Don and I walked over to the pancake breakfast. We crossed a unique covered bridge over a small stream. The rails on each side were made from tree trunks that had been washed down the river. At the end of each trunk was the tree's exposed root system. Each tree trunk was laid parallel to the bridge and crossed another tree trunk in the middle of the bridge, coming from a root system at the other end.

We walked out into a large open area with several picnic tables, a baseball field on one side, and an enclosed ice rink on the other. The breakfast was scheduled to be eaten outside, but a smattering of rain changed that. We picked up our plates of pancakes, sausage, baked beans, and Orange Tang drink and entered the arena to eat.

After we had eaten our fill, we went back to the hotel, where Dan had finished his shower. My first load of clothes was dry, and he had put my second load in the dryer. Don took his shower, and I headed back to camp, so Phil could have breakfast and a shower. By 11:00 a.m. the rain had stopped, and the wind had died down some.

During the afternoon we alternated trips to the barbecue. When Dan came down to relieve me from keeping watch over our camp, I went up, and Phil introduced me to Keith Hickling, the manager of Fish and Wildlife for the Sahtu Region. Keith had approached Phil, suspecting he was one of the paddlers camped down at the river. We invited him to visit our camp that evening.

At about 6:30 p.m. as Dan and I were standing on the shore of the river, two yellow canoes pulled ashore a few yards from our camp. The paddlers said hello and asked us where we had left from and where we were going. We found out they were part of the Northwest Territories Trans Canada Guidebook Project, "Connecting People, Land and Stories Through Traditional Trails." We met Jamie Basteda, who was the author and editor of the guidebook. When he learned I was planning to write a book about our expedition, he gave me his card and asked for my contact info, and we agreed to stay in touch and share information.

Jamie's group included a river guide named Carrie, who had paddled the Mackenzie twice previously, and two other guides, a man and a woman. All were very friendly, and we enjoyed meeting them and sharing experiences. We were all surprised that so few parties were traveling the river. They had seen two Europeans paddling birchbark canoes, but we were the only others they had seen. We agreed we would like to meet later downriver, but we were moving much quicker than them, and it was unlikely we would see them again.

From our position on the beach, the most striking features on the river were the six manmade islands with the rocker arms of pumps, pumping oil from under the river. These manmade islands allowed oil pumping year round.

Unlike most communities along the Mackenzie River, Norman Wells is not an historic settlement of the Déné. It began in the early 1900s when speculators filed oil claims. Eventually, the Imperial Oil Company purchased the claims and began drilling in 1911. A refinery was built, and the oil products were used by the surrounding communities for many years.

Alexander Mackenzie found oil seeping from the ground during his expedition in 1789. However, he wasn't the first person to discover oil in the area. The Aboriginals knew oil was there centuries before Mackenzie arrived. The Déné of the Sahtu Region named the area, "Le Gohlini" meaning "Where the Oil Is."

We stayed in camp and had beef stroganoff for dinner. As we were finishing, Keith Hickling stopped by. We spent a long time talking about our experiences on the river, and Keith shared information on the Sahtu Region. We showed him *The Sahtu Atlas* we had received from our friends, and he was astonished. He told us he had seen the book and had been trying to get a copy for himself but was finding it difficult. It seemed that only the Aboriginal people in the region had copies. We had felt honored when our friends presented us with the atlas, but after learning from Keith how rare it was for us to have a copy, we were even more appreciative.

Keith told us about a cabin built by Fish and Wildlife on Jackfish Creek, off the East Channel in the Mackenzie Delta. He said the cabin was available for our use if we were interested. I pulled out our maps, and Keith pinpointed the cabin.

I went into town to make one last contact with my family. I was able to reach Sue and all three of our grown children: John, Reed, and Melissa. At 9:45 I was in bed going over the maps and planning our departure from Norman Wells.

No miles traveled.

Campsite location: N65°16'44.3" W126°50'06.95"

EIGHTEEN
Uncle Wilfred

"The farther one gets into the wilderness, the greater is the attraction of its lonely freedom." – Theodore Roosevelt

Sunday, July 2, 2006 – Norman Wells to North of Patricia Island

We were all up by 6:00 a.m., fixing breakfast and breaking camp to get an early start. By 8:00 a.m. we pushed off the beach at Norman Wells and began paddling on flat water under clear skies. The river was swift, and with no headwind, we were able to paddle about 6 mph (10 kph).

At noon we paddled to the right of Ogilvie Island near Wilfred McDonald's home by Oscar Creek. On a long, wide gravel beach, we spotted stacks of firewood, recently split and put into piles in an area that was under water during and after breakup. It was an indication we were close to finding Uncle Wilfred. On a bluff above the beach was a cabin and a teepee, and sitting in a lawn chair watching us was Wilfred McDonald.

We landed, pulled our canoes up onto the beach, took off our life jackets, and walked to the bank as Wilfred watched us, saying nothing. When we climbed the bank and approached him, he looked at us hesitantly until we introduced ourselves and told him Lisa McDonald had asked us to stop by. The first words out of his mouth were, "Do you have any cigarettes?" None of us were smokers, but Phil, Don, and Dan did enjoy an occasional cigar, much to my displeasure.

Phil reached in his pocket and brought out a small pack of cigarillos. That broke the ice, and a pleasant smile replaced Wilfred's look of caution.

We chatted about Wilfred's experience living alone in the bush. He explained that he had been living there near Oscar Creek for eighteen years, and he was about to have his seventy-first birthday. I looked about and saw a nice cabin with a plywood exterior and windows with thick wire screens to keep the black bears out. "Bears have been a nuisance, but I've shot most of them," he said. The large yard was very neat with a freshly mowed lawn from his cabin to the surrounding forest. The teepee we had seen as we arrived had plywood on the exterior instead of the canvas we had seen on other teepees located along the river.

He invited us inside the cabin, and we found everything was clean, neat, and orderly. Wilfred told us about his life in the bush, shooting a moose each year in his yard and once through the screen door of his cabin. He explained that he heated and cooked with firewood he cut from logs brought down the river each year. He used to keep a trapline, but then he started setting traps in his yard and was able to "get some," as he put it. He said he saw a lynx the other day running across his yard. He set snares for rabbits, which he described as "good eatin'."

I commented on how neat his home and yard were and referred to his description of living alone in the wilderness. I told him it seemed to me that all he was missing was a good woman to keep him warm in the winter. With a twinkle in his eye, he told us that he'd had a couple of women who came to live with him at different times but complained they would move his stuff around and put their stuff in its place. He finished by saying, "The house wouldn't be so neat if there was a woman. I quit 'em."

He said he liked living there, but the winter road between Fort Good Hope and Norman Wells was close by, and he had to block the road into his yard. There wasn't a liquor store in Fort Good Hope, and during the winter the people traveled to Norman Wells on snowmobiles to get their booze. He said they stopped by on the way back "all juiced up."

"Then," he explained, "They want to eat up my food."

Back in the yard we broke out our lunch and continued to chat about the river and our expedition. During our conversation, Wilfred told us of a small spring along the river with good drinking water. His description was very comprehensive, and we were quite sure we would be able to spot it from the river.

We said goodbye and then walked down the bank, across the beach, past the wood piles, and to our canoes. We paddled past the end of Ogilvie Island and talked to two men who were camped at Oscar Creek. They said they had left from Norman Wells and tried to paddle up the creek to reach a waterfall, but the current was too swift, and they turned back. They were emptying their canoe, hoping a lighter canoe would make it easier to paddle against the current.

We paddled past Judith Island, Stanley Island, and Willard Island. We stopped at the head of Patricia Island, and Dan stepped out into deep mud, coming up well above his ankles. We had just passed a gravel beach, and Dan began plodding back toward it to find firmer ground.

Walking in the sticky mud was very difficult for Dan, and I watched him leaning far forward, using the weight of his upper body to help him pull his back foot out of the mud. I paddled the canoe upriver to meet Dan, and we were able to reach gravel, where we could sit and rest on a log. Although the gravel made walking easier, the beach was quite muddy and not a good location for our camp.

Dan pulled out his binoculars and looked north across the river toward the mainland. He spotted a beach he thought might be acceptable, and when Phil and Don arrived, we decided we would paddle across the river and check it out. Crossing there would require a forward ferry maneuver, pointing the bow slightly upriver and paddling hard to keep us moving toward the far shore but also moving against the current fast enough that we didn't move downriver. We pushed off with Phil and Don following close behind. We determined the angle and speed perfectly and landed in the exact location we had intended.

The beach near shore was strewn with large boulders, but closer to the bank was a stretch of moderately level gravel, large enough for our camp. Dan and Phil shared a beer, and Don and I shared a Coca-Cola. We set up camp and enjoyed a dinner of macaroni and cheese with Spam prepared by Chef Dan. It began to sprinkle as we set up camp, and by the time we ate dinner, a dark cloud came over us and dumped heavy rain on the Tundra tent while we ate. We celebrated the memorable day with a shot of Yukon Jack.

I was in my tent by 8:00 p.m. listening to the rain splatter against the fly. Fortunately, the fly did its job, and I stayed dry and comfortable.

33.2 mi (53.4 km) traveled today – 530.9 mi (854.4 km) overall

Campsite location: N65°33'05.9" W127°45'32.5"

NINETEEN
Sans Sault Rapids

"Life is either a daring adventure or nothing at all." – Helen Keller

Monday, July 3, 2006 – North of Patricia Island to 1.5 Miles (2.4 km) Past Dummit Islands

I woke up several times during the night as a series of heavy rain showers pelted my tent, and waves crashed on the beach. At 2:00 a.m. I looked out to see how the Tundra tent was holding up. One pole was down, and the stake that was supposed to be holding it up had pulled out. Everything underneath was still covered, so I decided to go back to sleep.

I had set my watch alarm for 5:00 a.m., so we could get an early start, but the sound of the waves kept me from hearing the alarm, and I didn't wake up until 6:15 a.m. I got up and re-staked the Tundra tent. The sound of me pounding the stake back in the ground woke the others. It was still raining, but the wind had died down. After breakfast we took down our tents and the Tundra tent, which were so heavy with water that I was sure we would be carrying an extra twenty pounds in the canoe.

Once on the water, as we passed the end of Patricia Island, the Coast Guard boat *Dumit* passed us on its way up the river. The captain gave us a toot, and the crew waved as they went by. I'm quite sure they knew who was on the water and radioed to the base in Hay River where and when they had seen us.

The river was moving swiftly, and we were making good time. We took our first break along Carcajou Ridge, just past Svenson Shoal. The ridge is a massive wall of colorful rock more than 8 mi (13 km) long. The water source Wilfred McDonald told us about was a small waterfall past the ridge and about 5 mi (8 km) from Carcajou River.

After our break we paddled across the Mackenzie and began looking for the waterfall. It was just as Wilfred had described, about 5 ft (1.5 m) wide, coming down a twenty–five-foot rocky bank and cascading into the river. This was the coldest, clearest water we had seen to that point. We pumped water into all our containers, washed up, and continued on.

We paddled between Axel Island and a small unnamed island to the west. Behind the small island is where the Carcajou River empties into the Mackenzie. We pulled onto a sandbar just beyond the Carcajou River to eat our lunch. Someone had been there recently because there were boot prints and a sand castle. We weren't aware of anyone paddling ahead of us, but we weren't too far from the village of Fort Good Hope, and at each of the villages we had passed, several open Lund aluminum boats were pulled up along the shore. It was likely someone from the village had stopped on the sandbar after the rain had stopped in the morning.

Just beyond the sandbar, we spent a half hour eating lunch and resting. Then we paddled out into the middle of the Mackenzie where the water was moving fast but without a ripple showing. My paddle suddenly hit the bottom, and I asked Dan to see if he was also hitting bottom. The water was so full of silt that it was impossible to see more than 2 in (5 cm) below the surface. Dan called back that it was getting shallow, and suddenly the canoe came to a stop with the water rushing by us. From my experience, most sandbars are relatively flat until you reach the end, where they drop sharply downward.

We stepped out of the canoe into about 4 in (10 cm) of water, which sloshed up against the back of our boots as we slowly pulled and pushed the canoe forward, constantly aware that we would eventually reach a drop-off. We developed a system of using our paddles to reach down into the water about 3 ft (0.9 m) in front before we took two steps. If we didn't reach the drop-off, we would pull the canoe forward. One missed step could result in a catastrophe, so we took our time and kept communicating the depth, the length of our pull, and any sign of a change in the water level. We continued in this manner for more than 100 ft (30 m) until Dan found the drop-off. He backed up and climbed into the canoe, using his paddle to keep the canoe pointed downriver as I pushed from the stern. When we estimated I was about 3 ft from the edge of the submerged bar, I climbed into the canoe, and we used our paddles to push off the bottom and into the main channel.

Phil and Don were behind us and, seeing our predicament, cut sharply to the right and were able to avoid running aground. As quickly as the river level was dropping, the sandbar would be completely exposed in twenty-four hours.

Moving water is a powerful force, and it's important to read the river to determine any hazards ahead. A large submerged rock can be identified by the movement above the water on the surface. Water will flow up and over the top of the rock, and this slight elevation of the water level can usually be spotted several hundred feet upriver. Trees hanging over the river are called sweepers because if you get too close, they can sweep you out of your canoe. When the water is high, the banks are undercut by the river. Trees washed into the current can become stuck on the river bottom with their root system piercing the surface. They are easy to spot and, on a wide river, easy to avoid. On narrower rivers, this is not so easy and may require walking along the shore to determine a safe passage through or a portage around the hazardous stretch.

Rapids occur where the river drops quickly, and waves of varying heights can give paddlers an exciting ride or a perilous experience. In some rapids, when the river is high, huge waves are formed and can swamp a canoe or capsize it. In high water the rocks and debris are sometimes so far below the surface that large waves aren't formed, and navigating the area isn't a problem. However, in the same location when the water is low, rocks and debris on the bottom are often exposed or are just under the surface and can present any number of hazards. Dan and I have paddled together through many different rapids on rivers throughout Canada, Alaska, Washington, Idaho, and Montana. It's a thrill to ride through rapids because the water moves so quickly, boiling and churning and causing the canoe to bounce around like a carnival ride. But safety is paramount, especially in the wilderness where no one is around to save you if you get into trouble. It's important to get as much information about rapids from people along the river and from books, pamphlets, and websites, if available. Regardless, approach rapids with caution, and scout them out first if at all possible.

The Sans Sault Rapids would be our first set of rapids on the Mackenzie, and anticipation was building throughout the day. Our friends living along the river advised us to stay to the left. We'd learned that the rapids were formed by a rocky ledge that extended from the north bank to the midpoint of the river. They said there was usually minimal turbulence on the left side of the river, so we stayed close to the left bank. As we heard the roar of the rapids ahead, our anxiety level began to rise. High on the left bank was a white monument in the shape of a teepee to honor a paddler, Hugh Donald Lockhart Gordon, who drowned in those rapids in 1961.

Suddenly, the river picked up speed, and we found ourselves headed directly toward a gravel bar. It came upon us so quickly that we had to make a snap decision to go left or right. We chose left but scraped the bottom of the canoe for an instant before being swept into the current alongside a steep, rocky half-mile-long bluff. We had successfully avoided the most dangerous portion of the rapids, thanks to our research and the advice of friends we met along the river.

We paddled close to a rocky beach to the left across from the Dummit Islands and drifted while we waited for Phil and Don. Several seagulls were perched side by side on a log high up on the beach. As we paddled close to shore, they rose up in a racket of squawks and began swooping down at us, letting us know we weren't wanted in their area. We assumed they had nests nearby that they were protecting.

When Phil and Don joined us, we decided it was time to begin looking for a camp spot. Dan pointed out a small island to the left, just past the Dummit Islands, that looked good from a distance. As we approached, we saw the beach was strewn with boulders. We continued on and found another possible site with fewer boulders and patches of wet, level sand. We had left in the morning before our tents were dry, and we wanted to pitch them soon, so they would dry in the wind. We were satisfied with the site and began to make camp. I lay my rain fly on bushes to keep it off the sand and in the wind. The rain had subsided during the day, but a dark cloud that seemed to be following us for much of the afternoon was moving in a southeast direction as the wind picked up.

Dinner was clam chowder followed by hot chocolate and cookies. The cloud we had been watching disappeared as the wind changed direction and began blowing downriver to the north. We hoped it would continue into the morning, so we could get an extra boost at our backs.

I went into my tent at about 9:00 p.m., read for a while, and wrote in my journal. The tent was dry, and the fly was secured to the tent in case of rain. It had been a good day of paddling, and the following day looked promising. I thought about Sue and all she had to do without me there to help. I missed her and reflected on how fortunate I was to have a wife who was willing to have me off in the wilderness for more than a month. She has always been very supportive of my adventures and has even joined me on some. I'm very lucky!

41 mi (66 km) traveled today – 571.9 mi (920.4 km) overall

Campsite location: N65°47'01.1" W128°49'44.5"

TWENTY
The Ramparts

"We need the sweet pain of anticipation to tell us we are really alive." – Albert Camus (French Algerian philosopher, author, and journalist)

Tuesday, July 4, 2006 – 1.5 Miles (2.4 km) Past Dummit Islands to Hare Indian River

My tent was very warm when I woke up at 5:30 a.m. The sun was shining, and a wind was blowing downriver. As I stuffed my sleeping bag and rolled up my Thermarest mattress, I heard the others begin to stir.

I grabbed my camera and walked down the beach with the warm wind at my back, enjoying the moment. A few hundred feet from camp, I saw tracks in the soft mud—footprints from a large wolf. The mud was soft but dried to a thin crust on the surface. The tracks were pressed down into the damp mud underneath, which meant they could be only hours old. I looked around, carefully observing to see if the wolf was still within sight. I doubted it was but thought it best to stay alert.

I walked back to camp, where the others were all up, and told them what I had seen. We all walked down the beach, so I could show them the tracks.

At 8:00 a.m. we were on the river, heading toward the Ramparts, purported by some to be the most challenging rapids north of Great Slave Lake. We had been able to avoid the Sans Sault Rapids by staying to the far left, but through my study prior to the trip, I learned that at the Ramparts, high cliffs, 180 to 300 ft (55 to 91 m) tall, come straight down to the water on both sides of the river, with no ledges or beaches to land on in case of trouble. Alexander Mackenzie was warned by Aboriginals to fear those rapids, which had claimed the lives of many in the past. Anticipation and some apprehension were building as we paddled closer to the well-known 7-mile (11-km) stretch.

In 1789 when Alexander McKenzie was leading an expedition down the river, he encountered many small groups of "Natives" along the banks who escaped into the woods as soon as they saw these strange river travelers. The guides, which he called "conductors," were local Déné who he had persuaded to lead his expedition down the river. The conductors called to the slowest of the Aboriginals retreating from the shoreline and convinced most of them to return, assuring them they had nothing to fear from the visitors. After meeting Mackenzie and his party, they convinced most of the others to return as well. Mackenzie gave them knives, beads, awls, and other items. In return, Mackenzie was presented with fish, fowl, and hares.

Mackenzie reached the area during the same week in July that we arrived. I assumed the water levels would have been similar because many of Mackenzie's descriptions of the river were similar to what we had been seeing. He traveled across the river and paddled along the western shore where he skirted the Sans Sault Rapids. He wrote in his journal that this was one of the dangerous rapids he had been warned about but the easy passage ". . . convinced me in my Opinion respecting the falsity of the Native Information." He even wrote, ". . . we might have saved ourselves the trouble as there was no danger in going straight down it." Perhaps the water level was higher during Mackenzie's expedition because the whitewater and roar of the rapids convinced me that we could not have safely gone straight down the rapids.

The speed of the river helped keep our speed around 7 mi (11 km) per hour throughout the morning. Just before we arrived at the Hume River, we crossed to the east side, which we thought would be the best place from which to enter the rapids. Perhaps we should have waited to cross until we passed the mouth of the Hume River and Hume Island because we encountered a series of sandbars that trapped us in shallow water and forced us to paddle upriver several times in order to find a passage between the bars. When we reached Hume Island, we began looking for a good landing spot, so we could rest and eat lunch before our 7.5-mile (12-km) paddle through the canyon.

As we passed the north end of the island, we paddled by the camp of two Déné men. A half mile farther, we found a good place to stop for lunch. We decided to open a couple of MREs we had packed for times when we wanted a warm meal but didn't want to go through the long process of preparing a meal.

We purchased most of our food from grocery stores. We bought vegetables in villages where they were available, but most of our food was dried, packaged food or canned goods that would stay preserved in our watertight dry bags or containers. However, before we started our trip, we did purchase some surplus military provisions, called MREs or Meals Ready to Eat. We hadn't yet opened any, but we didn't want to carry them home, so we pulled out two meals: ravioli dinner and macaroni and cheese with chili. MREs include the main course as well as a side dish, such as corn, rice, fruit, or mashed potatoes. Bread or crackers are included along with a spread, such as peanut butter, jelly, or cheese spread. A dessert, such as cookies, pound cake or candy (M&Ms, Skittles, or Tootsie Rolls) finish out the meal. Utensils are provided along with hot sauce and other seasonings, matches, toilet paper, and chewing gum. A flameless heat packet is included to heat up the main course.

We enjoyed our MREs and marveled at how they were able to get so much in such a small package. I'm not sure if we would have enjoyed the military meals in the comfort of our homes, but they were quite tasty sitting on the side of the second-largest river in North America after three weeks in the wilderness.

The suspense was building as we considered what we might face in the Ramparts. Some accounts I had read warned of the dangers we would face while others remarked at how little whitewater there was. The river was high but had dropped considerably in the past two weeks. Did that mean we would be more likely or less likely to face a raging torrent through the canyon? We made sure all our gear was tied down securely to the D-rings I had installed in the bottom of the canoe, and we secured the spray skirt tightly to the loops along the sides of the canoe.

We left our lunch spot and passed Spruce Island, the last island before entering the Ramparts. At the north end of the island, the river was approximately 1.25 mi (2 km) wide. The entrance to the Ramparts was a little more than 328 ft (100 m) wide. The narrowing of the river meant that a massive amount of water was being pushed through the narrow canyon. Alexander Mackenzie took soundings when he passed through and found a depth of 50 fathoms or 300 ft (91 m) at one location. Further measurements have found depths as much as 360 ft (110 m).

While paddling along the eastern shore, we heard a roar in the distance, which added to our anxiety. The sound of whitewater is unmistakable, and we wanted to be sure we were completely prepared for whatever we faced. We saw the end of a white limestone cliff on the eastern side of the entrance but were unable to look around a limestone point and into the narrow opening. We decided to make one more stop and pulled alongside a rockslide that Dan had seen from a distance. We thought it might be a snowfield, but as we came closer, we saw it consisted of white limestone rock. We stopped and made one last check of our lashings before heading to the point and entering the canyon.

As we approached the entrance, the sound of the rushing water we had heard earlier was to our left. We paddled closer and discovered the sound was not coming from rapids but from water rushing around one of the Coast Guard buoys. As we rounded the point, prepared to choose a route through the tumult, we were shocked to see flat water. It was swift and boiling in some spots, but there was no whitewater, no waves, and no danger. What we saw was a spectacular canyon with sheer walls of limestone reaching to heights from 180 to 300 ft (55 to 91 m). The cliffs showed evidence of erosion, and we saw several rocks tumble down from the cliffs and into the water. We were moving faster than anywhere else on the river up to that point. The rock walls showed striations from thousands of years of deposits, and the river had undercut the cliffs in many locations, the top layers stretching out 15 ft (4.6 m) or more over the river. The land at the top of the cliffs was flat and brushy with numerous spires of black spruce trees rising from the ground. Streams from melting spring snow had cut small gullies into the rock. Loose rock and gravel sliding around firmer rock had created hoodoos throughout the 7-mile (11-km) canyon. Swallows, terns, and seagulls played in the wind above the water. We laid our paddles on the floor of the canoe, leaned against the backrests of our seats, and relaxed, enjoying the splendor of the canyon.

The river took a turn to the right, and as we turned, we saw the village of Fort Good Hope in the distance. A church spire stood above all the other buildings. We landed at the boat launch at 4:30 p.m., about a mile ahead of Phil and Don. Dan and I walked up and checked in with the RCMP and used their phone to call home. Dan walked down to the canoe to wait for Phil and Don, and I walked up the street, looking for the local store. I passed the church and the cemetery with white picket fences around each of the family plots. I hoped to stop and take a look inside the church on the way back. I found the store, but it was about to close, and the staff made it clear they wanted me to leave. I grabbed a bottle of Coca-Cola, a small bag of Fritos, and a can of Pringles, costing more than $15.

In my research I had learned about Our Lady of Good Hope Church, which had become a legend throughout the region. In 1859, Father Pierre-Henri Grollier opened a Roman Catholic mission in the community. Fort Good Hope was established by the Hudson's Bay Company at the turn of the nineteenth century. Construction of the church took twenty years, beginning in 1865, and was completed in 1885. Father Emile Petitot arrived during construction and began painting murals on the walls. Other artists from the area added additional murals. In 1978, the church was registered as a historic site.

I hiked down toward the boat launch and stopped to see if we would be able to see the inside of this famous church. I was disappointed to find it was closed for the day. The pictures I had seen on the internet were spectacular. I continued walking to the canoes and shared my Coke and snacks with Dan. I shouldn't have let the people in the store rush me, and I should have purchased more Coke, something the others didn't hesitate to tell me.

When Phil and Don arrived, they walked up to the RCMP office and called home while Dan and I waited with the canoes. When they returned we discussed whether we should spend the night in the village. Since the church and the store were closed, and we couldn't see an appropriate location to set up camp, we decided there was little left for us in Fort Good Hope, so we left the village and paddled on.

Three miles (5 km) downriver we reached the mouth of Hare Indian River. It was shown as Hare Indian River on our map, but our friends along the river called it Rabbit Skin River. We found an adequate camping location just past the river. We set up our tents and raised the Tundra tent just in time for a rain shower to arrive.

47.4 mi (76.3 km) traveled today – 619.3 mi (996.7 km) overall

Campsite location: N66°17'47.2" W128°37'46.9"

TWENTY-ONE
Crossing the Arctic Circle

"The cold cut like a many bladed knife." – Israel Zangwill (British author)

Wednesday, July 5, 2006 – Indian Hare River to 6 Miles (9.7 km) North of the Arctic Circle

The tent was nearly dry when I awakened at 7:00 a.m. The previous day it hadn't rained other than the short shower just after we arrived at our camp. After we took down our tents and loaded all our gear into the canoe, we pumped water from the Hare Indian River. The water was clear and silt free, so we weren't concerned about our pump filters.

By 9:30 a.m. we were back on the Mackenzie. Beyond Fort Good Hope, the river had become wide again, and it continued to flow at a speed that allowed us to make good time, even though we were constantly battling headwinds.

By the time we stopped for lunch at 11:30 a.m., we had traveled 11 mi (18 km) at approximately 5.5 mi (9 km) per hour. We landed on a point of land just beyond two small islands. The beach was different from any of the previous beaches. Rocks averaging 3 to 4 in (7 to 12 cm) in diameter, worn smooth by the river, were laid out from the bank to the shore in a smooth array like a cobblestone street.

The temperature had dropped during the morning. After taking off my life jacket, I became chilled, so I built a fire using small pieces of driftwood. Firewood was prevalent now that the river had dropped. The combination of long days of sun and wind had dried the wood, so it ignited quickly. Dan brought out venison pepperoni sticks, and Don and I found some small branches, so we could roast them over the coals like hot dogs.

The sky was overcast, and dark rain clouds hung over the valley to the north. We seemed to be a magnet for storms. We hadn't experienced more than two days between storms, and it looked like we were headed for another. We passed on the right of a long unnamed island. As soon as we paddled around the protection of that island, the wind hit us head on, and we saw large black clouds assembling in front of us. It was not a storm we wanted to face on the water, so we headed for shore. We built a lean-to out of driftwood poles and finished stretching my red tarp over the top only seconds before the rain hit. The tarp was pelted by large drops that created a loud drumming sound, but we stayed dry. Twenty minutes later the intense rain subsided. We were eager to move on, so we removed the tarp from the lean-to and left the frame on the beach for other river travelers.

Back on the river, the rain diminished to a few sprinkles, but soon the dark clouds released another surge of rain, just as we crossed the Arctic Circle. I wanted to take a picture to commemorate the crossing, but I wasn't willing to risk my camera getting wet.

Our spray skirts covering the canoe helped to keep most of the water out, but as the wind blew and the rain bombarded us, water began to seep through the nylon. Some of the waves came up and over the canoe, but most of the water rolled off. Because I was in the stern seat and weighed more than Dan, any water that got into the canoe flowed back to me. Every so often I had to stop paddling and bail as Dan kept us pointing into the waves.

My rain suit wasn't keeping the rain from soaking through, and I was sweating because I was paddling so vigorously. The temperature was dropping, and I was beginning to get cold. The wind was pushing the rain in sheets toward us, and my legs started to become numb. I had thin gloves on my hands, and I was holding the paddle tightly to get the most from my stroke. Frequently, I moved my fingers to keep the circulation going, but it took several attempts before my fingers would flex normally.

We passed the Tieda River where the Noels stayed in a cabin, but we were so busy trying to move forward and stay afloat that we didn't see the cabin or the river. After several miles of digging in and fighting the wind and waves, my clothes were soaked. Water kept coming into the canoe, and I had to bail more often. I yelled to Dan to look for a place to land, so we could build a fire and put up a shelter. Phil and Don were close enough that we could see them but not close enough to communicate. I wasn't sure how they were doing but suspected they were also wet and cold. I started to think about hypothermia but believed if I kept paddling briskly, my body would produce the heat I needed.

After rounding a point of land, Dan spotted a cabin. We carefully turned the canoe, so we could cross the waves at a 45-degree angle, moving forward but not allowing the waves to hit us broadside. Phil and Don did the same, and we all landed on the beach below the cabin at about the same time.

I stepped onto the beach but struggled to stand. I was cold and exhausted. Once I stood and moved around a bit, I regained my balance. We pulled the canoe up over large boulders and tied it to a log on the shore. Dan and I climbed the steep bank. There wasn't much of a trail—more of a small gully where running water had eroded the bank. It was slippery, and we struggled to reach the top.

Once on the flat surface above the bank, we saw not only the cabin but also a large Fort McPherson wall tent. We tried the cabin first, but the door was padlocked. We weren't sure of the condition of the wall tent and whether it could shelter us from the storm. The canvas on the front end of the tent, facing the river, was split down the middle, forming two flaps that were laced together. I stepped onto an improvised step and attempted to unlace the flaps, so we could see inside. My fingers were so numb that I struggled with the cord, so Dan joined in. Once I could see inside the tent, I let out a whoop because the wooden floor was completely dry, and there was a bed with metal springs (no mattress), a table, and a chair. It wasn't much, but in our condition, it was magnificent.

Dan and I walked back to the edge of the bank overlooking the river and told Phil and Don what we had found. We walked down the bank to collect our gear, slipping and sliding on the steep, muddy trail. After several trips up the bank with our precious supplies and equipment, we were ready to settle in, get into dry clothes, and find a way to warm our bodies.

Dan claimed the bed, and Phil, Don, and I laid out our Thermarest mattresses and sleeping bags. Thanks to our dry bags, our extra clothes and sleeping gear weren't wet. We changed our clothes and laid our wet things around the tent, so they could dry. There was a small stove in the northwest corner, just below a round opening in the tent wall for a chimney. We found several pieces of metal chimney and pieced them together, using an elbow piece to form a right angle, so the pipe could go horizontally out through the hole in the tent.

PERSEVERANCE

We started a fire with some dry wood stacked near the stove. The fire took hold quickly and started radiating heat immediately. We crowded around the stove and pulled out our bottle of Yukon Jack to toast our fortunate discovery.

The wood in the tent wasn't enough to keep the fire going all night, so we walked down to the beach and brought back armloads of driftwood. Even though the wood was wet on the outside, it was dry enough under the outside layer to keep the fire crackling. The heat warmed our bodies and started to dry out our clothes. The tent canvas allowed light to penetrate, so we had no trouble seeing.

We had no knowledge of whom the tent belonged to, but we had little doubt the owners would be okay with us staying there as long as we left it in as good a condition as we found it. On the Yukon River, we had found cabins with notes posted welcoming us but to keep them clean and protected. No such note was posted at that spot, but there was a code in the wilderness of Alaska when I lived there that those in need of shelter were welcome to stay in remote cabins as needs arose. I assumed that was the case there.

Don cooked lasagna for dinner, and we finished with cookies and another shot of Yukon Jack. After dinner we sat on our camp chairs and reminisced about our struggles on the river and our luck in finding that shelter. Eventually, we banked up the fire and climbed into our sleeping bags.

Just as we were about to fall asleep, the tent began to fill with smoke. Dan and I got up to discover that the wind had changed direction and was blowing directly into the stove pipe. We needed another elbow and section of pipe going straight up outside the tent to pull the smoke away from the chimney. Unfortunately, we couldn't find an elbow or another section of chimney. We couldn't keep breathing the heavy smoke, so we let the fire die out. Phil opened the flap, and the wind rushed in, dispersing most of the smoke. Eventually, he closed the flap, and we all climbed back into our sleeping bags. The temperature dropped quickly, but we were prepared for sleeping in cold weather, and our sleeping bags and fleece liners kept us snug throughout the night.

26.3 mi (42.3 km) traveled today – 645.6 mi (1039 km) overall

Campsite location: N66°33'8.29" W129°12'8.42"

TWENTY-TWO
A Better Day

"It is pleasant to have been to a place the way a river went." – Henry David Thoreau

Thursday, July 6, 2006 – Six Miles (9.7 km) North of the Arctic Circle to 8 Miles (12.9 km) North of Ontaratue River

Morning was very cold, and I was reluctant to climb out of my sleeping bag; my fleece liner was helping to keep me warm and comfortable. Phil had left a narrow space between the flaps at the end of the wall tent to allow fresh air in and to drive the smoke out. With the coals in the stove completely out, the inside air was clear and cold. Only my face was exposed, and with each breath, a puff of fog materialized and quickly dispersed. Thankfully, we had spent a very comfortable night out of the rain and were happy to have survived the wind, waves, rain, and chill of the previous day. When the body is cold, it generally stays cold for a long time unless it is exposed to an external heat source. The shelter of the tent was important, but the heat from the stove was critical. My body was warm and dry when I entered my sleeping bag, and I stayed warm throughout the night.

Phil was the first one up, and by the time I dragged myself out of the sack, he was making coffee. I don't generally drink coffee, but the smell was irresistible. The temperature inside was 41°F (5°C). I had no doubt it was near freezing outside during the night.

PERSEVERANCE

Don was soon up and dressed, wearing a hat I hadn't yet seen. It had flaps on both sides to cover his ears, and he looked like a long-eared dog. I jokingly told him he looked like a dork. "But I'm a warm dork," he replied with a big grin.

The hot oatmeal we fixed for breakfast boosted our spirits and charged our bodies with energy and warmth. We stuffed our dry bags and dry boxes and made several trips down to the canoes. Dan wrote a note to the owners of the tent on a piece of paper from his journal. He described our need to use their tent and thanked them for its accessibility. He also left a paperback book to add to those already on the table. We collected more firewood from the beach, dryer now that it hadn't rained for several hours, and made sure we left at least twice as much as we had burned. We swept the floor and made sure everything was neat and clean before we left.

By 7:30 a.m. we had lashed our gear in the canoes and tied down the spray skirts we had dried overnight in the tent. I put on a flannel shirt and a wool sweater, determined to stay warm. In the distance we could see a rain shower, but when we left we were dry and warm.

The Mackenzie River Valley, like most large river valleys, is generally wide and flat above the riverbanks. Much of the land around the Mackenzie River is peppered with swamps, ponds, and lakes. The terrain throughout the far north generally consists of muskeg, a boggy mixture of water and decaying vegetation covered by sphagnum or other mosses. Deciduous trees, including birch, balsam poplar, and willow are found along the shores of lakes and rivers. The black spruce trees, so common to the Arctic, become shorter and spindlier the farther north they grow. This is due to longer, colder winter weather and permanently frozen soil, known as permafrost, that begins just inches below the surface.

Northerners often take advantage of the permafrost, digging down into the frozen soil to create a freezer for meat and vegetables. When Dan, Phil, and I paddled down the Yukon River from Whitehorse in the Yukon Territory to Circle City, AK, in 2001, we visited two men who lived along the river. They showed us the inside of a cabin on the site, lifted the floorboards, and exposed a defunct chest freezer buried in the permafrost. Everything inside the freezer was frozen solid. No electricity needed!

We paddled under cloudy skies with occasional sunny breaks. It was the coldest day yet, but we were better prepared for the cold than we were for the hot weather at the beginning of our expedition. As we paddled to the left side of the Askew Islands, we pulled ashore along the west bank of the river to rest.

We had found that a short break every two hours was needed to rest our arms and walk off the stiffness in our legs. Sitting in one position for two hours with our legs limited to the narrow confines of the canoe could result in restless legs and cramps. Standing and walking for even a few minutes every couple of hours helped immensely.

When Phil and Don saw that we were stopped on the west bank, they were very close to the Askew Islands. It would have been difficult to cross the swiftly moving river to join us, so they landed on a small beach along one of the islands.

After our break we paddled for another two hours before stopping for lunch. I built a fire on the gravel beach, and we stood warming our legs and hands. Dan dug into his dry bag and brought out pepperoni to roast over the fire. Small drops of melted fat oozed out and dropped onto the fire with a sizzle and a puff of smoke that filled the air with a delightful aroma.

After leaving our lunch spot, we paddled into the current and spent a generally uneventful afternoon on the river. The weather remained cold, and the sun appeared occasionally from behind high clouds.

When we approached islands, we were faced with a decision to go left or right. On smaller rivers, the decision of which side of an island to take can keep you in the current, swiftly moving down the river, or it can lead you into shallow water or a dead end, with the river moving through piles of logs and other debris. On a large, wide river like the Mackenzie, the water on either side of an island is usually wide and clear, but the water on one side might flow faster than the other.

Dan and I tried to read the river to choose the fastest route. As we approached an island, we weighed the pros and cons of one side versus the other. The river was moving faster in some areas than others, and we became better at making these decisions with more experience. Phil and Don were doing the same, and sometimes they found faster water and easily left us behind while at other times we found the faster water. It became a friendly competition to see who was better at reading the river. Phil was experienced with several years of river paddling, but this was Don's first river paddle. After three weeks on the Mackenzie, however, Don was becoming more skilled at recognizing the characteristics of the current.

My back was hurting because of the way I had slept on it, and the sharp pain in my neck had become worse throughout the day. Whenever it was necessary to dig in and paddle faster, the pain increased. Phil was complaining about a similar pain in his neck, and Don was experiencing several aches and pains. We were all feeling the results of fatigue.

After 35 mi (56 km), we were ready to end our paddling for the day. No longer did we have to hunt for a suitable campsite, because they were plentiful now that the river had dropped so much. We became selective. Suitable wasn't good enough. Our standards had changed, and only the best would do. (This reminded me of one of our family camping trips when I worried the entire way whether we would be able to find a campsite in the state park—any campsite. Once we arrived and found half the park empty, we drove around analyzing each available spot before we picked the best one.)

We came to a small point of land and saw the optimum site for our camp. The beach consisted of rocky spots with sandy stretches between and a small stream coming down into the river. We each found excellent locations for our tents and then selected a good spot in front of a log for the Tundra tent. The wind was blowing hard, so we tied the back of the Tundra tent to the log to keep it secure. The clouds that had stayed with us most of the day were almost gone, and the sun was keeping us warmer—much warmer than the previous day. The deciduous trees rustled in the wind as we shared a Coca-Cola. We ate dinner and spent the evening in the Tundra tent. There was something special about that campsite that I can't explain. As the sun dipped toward the horizon, the netting flopped and billowed in the wind. We sat in our camp chairs and ate dinner, sharing the highlights of the day.

35.3 mi (56.8 km) traveled today – 680.9 mi (1095.8 km) overall

Campsite location: N66°53'7.16" W130°7'9.38"

RCMP officer Mike Jordan on his day off in Tulita

Three young boys welcoming us to Tulita

PERSEVERANCE

A portion of the old Hudson's Bay post in Tulita

Look carefully to see the three giant beaver pelts on the side of the mountain

Don showing off his canoe with Ox the "ugly" stuffed animal at the bow

Waiting out a storm south of Prohibition Creek

Georgie McKay and Ron at Canada Day party

PERSEVERANCE

Georgie and Phil at Canada Day party

Foot bridge in Norman Wells

Canada Day barbecue in Norman Wells

Learning about the Mackenzie Delta from Keith Hickling

PERSEVERANCE

Wilfred McDonald at his Oscar Creek cabin

Eating lunch and visiting with Wilfred McDonald

Collecting water from small waterfall recommend by Wilfred

John's Walrus tent pitched on a muddy beach near the Ramparts

PERSEVERANCE

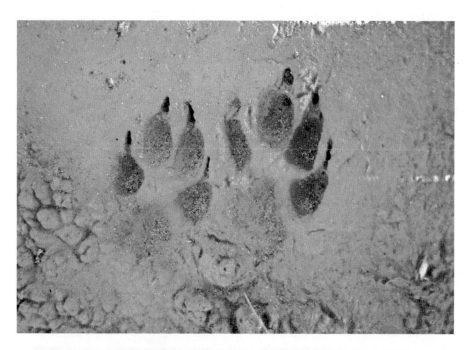

Recent paw prints from a very large wolf

High anticipation entering the Ramparts

PERSEVERANCE

Our surprise to find flat water in the Ramparts

Hoodoos on the left side of the Ramparts

Phil making a point

PERSEVERANCE

Dan and John in front of the sandstone canyon walls of the Ramparts

John R. Richardson

Our Lady of Good Hope Church in Fort Good Hope

PERSEVERANCE

Roasting pepperoni for lunch

Don preparing bannock and cake for dinner using his backpacker oven

TWENTY-THREE
Little Chicago

"This river's taught me a good bit. Probably why I don't leave here. It winds, weaves, snakes around. Rarely goes the same way twice. But, in the end, it always ends up in the same place and the gift is never the same . . . It's the journey that matters." – Charles Martin in Where the River Ends

Friday, July 7, 2006 – 8 Miles (12.9 km) North of Ontaratue River to a Point 12 Miles (19.3 km) Past Little Chicago

The weather turned cold during the night, and I awoke at 1:30 a.m. when my sleeping bag wasn't keeping me warm. I pulled my fleece liner from its stuff bag and worked it into my sleeping bag. During those few minutes out of the bag, my already-cold body became even colder. By the time I slipped back inside, I was shivering, and since a sleeping bag is not designed to heat up the body, it took a long time for my interior warmth to radiate to my cold exterior. I was still cold when I fell asleep forty-five minutes later.

When I woke up at 6:00 a.m., I was warm and comfortable and reluctantly crawled out of my sleeping bag as I heard the others unzipping their tents. We hustled around dismantling our tents and stuffing dry bags. After a quick breakfast of oatmeal and breakfast bars, we loaded the canoes and were on the water by 8:00 a.m.

The river was approximately 2.5 mi (4 km) wide at that point, and we could see for several miles down the long stretch. That broad section seemed more like a lake than a river. There was no wind, so the surface was tranquil with only an

PERSEVERANCE

occasional small boil created from the movement of the water. I haven't enjoyed paddling large lakes as much as rivers, because they are not as engaging. The movement of a river presents challenges that require constant vigilance. A small fast-moving river presents an even greater challenge, keeping my mind focused on the water, looking for signs of danger, and making quick adjustments.

As we continued through the calm water, my mind wandered to the world I had left behind, to my kids, my grandkids, and my wife. Sue had taken over my duties and responsibilities while I pursued this journey. I thought of how fortunate I was to have a wife, my best friend, who supported my dreams and objectives.

I retired after a thirty-five-year career as a teacher and school principal. One week after retirement, I left for Whitehorse to fulfill a decades-old dream of paddling the Yukon River. Dan, Phil, and Gary Mowry, the father-in-law of my son, Reed, joined me on a 700-mile (1,127-km) expedition from Whitehorse to Circle City, AK. When I returned home, I began a second career as an educational consultant. One of my contracts was with the State of Washington, facilitating school improvement in three elementary schools and one middle school. I was one of several school improvement facilitators who worked with teachers and principals to help them develop and implement strategies to improve the learning of their students.

Although each facilitator worked independently in different schools, we met frequently throughout each year and one week during each summer to learn from each other's experiences and review the latest research findings on student learning. I was missing the summer meeting while I was on our expedition, but I learned later that my colleagues were thinking of me and even raised a toast to my safety at one of their dinners.

One of the most crucial elements of a successful school—or any organization or system—is good leadership. I thought about this in relationship to our canoe trip as I paddled down that quiet section of river. The paddler in the stern is generally responsible for guiding the direction of the canoe. Both paddlers use the most basic stroke for forward power, the forward stroke. This stroke keeps the canoe in a straight line. The backward stroke is used when backing away from shore and into the current. A variety of different strokes are used for turning or correcting, including the J-stroke, the forward or reverse sweep, the draw, and the pry. These can be used by either paddler, but they have the most effect when used by the stern paddler. The bow paddler's primary responsibility is to use the forward stroke to provide power.

Working together, the paddlers keep the canoe moving toward the destination in the most efficient manner. One might consider the stern paddler as the leader because he is responsible for steering the craft toward the desired objective, much like a leader in any system is responsible for steering the organization toward the desired objective. However, the leader has to rely on input from others in the system for data to be used in successful steering. In the canoe I constantly relied on Dan to tell me what he saw ahead since he had a closer, unobstructed view forward. He would tell me if there was a rock, a submerged log, or other obstruction ahead, so I could make the necessary adjustments. In my school I expected my staff to alert me to problems, such as an angry parent, an out-of-control student, or a strategy that wasn't working, so I could make a correction. In each case, if the type of correction isn't obvious, a discussion of possible corrections and expected results makes for a more successful outcome. Therefore, a successful leader is not a "boss" but a facilitator. In the same way, the bow paddler isn't there just to provide power but is a critical member of the team, sharing in decisions and receiving the rewards of success.

We took our first break on a gravel beach consisting of rocks worn smooth by the movement of the water and sand. The rocks ranged in color from white to black with almost every color imaginable. Phil, Dan, and I walked the beach, looking for just the right ones to add to a collection of feathers, driftwood, and other interesting items we were finding on our expedition. Don playfully made disparaging remarks about the weight we were adding to our canoes, hoping Dan's and my rocks would slow us down and threatening to throw Phil's in the river.

The weather was still cold, but the sun was shining. We left our gravel beach and continued on. We passed the site of Little Chicago, an abandoned community first settled by prospectors in 1897.

The would-be prospectors who settled in Little Chicago were among those encouraged by unscrupulous businessmen in Edmonton to follow an overland trail up the Peel River to the Klondike gold fields. They were told that the route was suitable all winter, but on their way down the Mackenzie, the river froze before they reached the Peel, and they had to spend the winter along the Mackenzie. Several of these men were from Chicago, so they named the community "Little Chicago." They spent the winter trapping and were so successful that several gave up their quest for gold and remained at the site for several years. There is no trace of the community today.

PERSEVERANCE

We stopped for lunch at another gravel beach and found more rocks to add to our collection. We finished our day of paddling about 18 mi (29 km) past Little Chicago, landing on an 80-foot-long (24 m) mostly gravel beach with several sandy patches. When we landed, a peregrine falcon began screeching at us, and another joined in the racket. There was likely a nest nearby. Near the bank were several level sandy spots, where we pitched our tents. The hillside at the back of our camp consisted of sand and gravel about 80 to 100 ft (24 to 30 m) high.

As we pitched our tents, a loon sounded its mournful call from the river. Fred Morton, a close Canadian friend who has spent his entire life living and working along the British Columbia coast, claims this sound is a warning that the weather is about to change.

Once again we had found a superb campsite. Clouds were scattered across the sky with plentiful areas of sunlight. The opposite shoreline, a mile and a half away, and the hillside above it were reflected in a perfect image on the river's flat, undisturbed surface. The sun appeared occasionally through the cumulus clouds, reflecting warmth to everything surrounding our camp.

38.4 mi (61.8 km) traveled today – 719.3 mi (1157.6 km) overall

Campsite location: N67°20'29.1" W130°42'6.80"

TWENTY-FOUR
Travaillant River

"Rivers run through our history and folklore, and link us as a people." – Charles Kuralt (American journalist)

Saturday, July 8, 2006 – A Point 12 Miles (19.3 km) Past Little Chicago to 10 mi (16.1 km) Past Travaillant River

We spent another cold night on the shore of the river. The peregrine falcons renewed their protests as we began to stir at 6:00 a.m. They squawked and swooped around our camp, letting us know once again that we weren't welcome. These birds can fly with remarkable swiftness, reaching speeds of over 200 mi (322 km) per hour.

I woke up earlier, at 3:00 a.m., with the wind blowing downriver and ruffling my tent. I had hoped the wind might be at our backs once we began paddling, but it died down completely by the time I got out of the tent. I saw a few clouds to the southwest, but the sky above us was clear.

We each took our turn using the satellite phone, checking in with our families. We kept our conversations short because of the cost. I was able to reach Sue, and she was happy to hear that we were progressing safely.

Finding a good campsite had become much easier in recent days. We looked for relatively level ground, free of mud and sharp rocks. A gravel or sandy beach was excellent, easy to smooth out if necessary and soft enough to allow our tent stakes to penetrate but firm enough to hold. Because the Tundra tent had such a large surface area, it could catch the wind and collapse easily. Whenever possible, we tried to anchor it to a log.

At 7:00 a.m. the sun began to work over the cliff above our camp. Sunlight hit the lower part of the beach and quickly worked its way up to our campsite while we were eating breakfast. We loaded our canoes, and while Dan and I were lashing down our gear, Phil and Don shoved off. Ten minutes later we left the shore, but they had a good head start and must have caught the current just right, because it took us longer than usual to get close.

We approached the first big bend in the river, choosing the left center while Phil and Don stayed left, closer to the beach. Just ahead of us, a sandbar materialized suddenly, and we were forced to pass it on the right in slower water. Don and Phil caught another fast section, and suddenly the distance between us grew. We paddled a good half mile before we found fast water, and by that time they were almost out of sight.

After two hours of paddling, Phil and Don found a good rest spot and landed five minutes ahead of us. The beach was another treasure trove of rocks, many with striations varying in color and texture. I added a few to my collection, as did Dan and Phil. Don did his usual grumbling about the extra weight and once again threatened to throw Phil's rocks out of the canoe. Phil just smiled and continued to add more specimens to his collection. Our rock supply was growing, and we considered stashing them close to the road at Tsiigehtchic, formerly known as Arctic Red River. We would be driving back from Inuvik on the Dempster Highway and could pick them up after our ferry crossing.

During the planning of this expedition, we considered different means of getting our canoes back to Inuvik if we paddled to Tuktoyaktuk on the Arctic Ocean. We thought of paddling back from Tuk but determined the currents would make it too difficult. NTCL, the barge company that was transporting my truck to Inuvik, also served Tuk, but their barge schedule and our timeline weren't compatible. We decided to wait until we reached Inuvik where we hoped to find someone with a boat who could meet us in Tuk and transport the canoes and gear back to Inuvik.

At our rest stop, Phil and Don told us they weren't motivated to paddle from Inuvik to Tuk. Dan suggested that if we could find someone willing to rent a boat to Phil and Don, they could run the boat down to Tuk and meet us there. If we couldn't find someone willing to rent them a boat, perhaps we could find someone willing to make the journey down to Tuk with Phil and Don to bring the canoe back. Either way, they could see the Arctic Ocean without having to paddle that extra distance. Everyone agreed this was a good solution. The challenge would be finding someone with a boat who would agree to help us.

We stopped at the Travaillant River for lunch.

While planning the expedition, I found one account about how schooners were used on the lower Mackenzie. The mouth of the Travaillant River was used to store at least one schooner during the winter. Using a capstan and winches, the schooner was pulled up to higher ground at a site up the Travaillant. In the late 1920s, William (Billy) Clark was the first person to build a permanent structure at this location which soon became an independent trading post and was open for business between 1927 and 1939. Trappers along the Travaillant and its tributaries would come to Clark's post for supplies. Bill McNeely bought the camp from Clark in 1942 and opened his own trading post, which endured until 1956.

After lunch, Dan and I took a walk, looking for any sign of the old trading post. We climbed a small bank and walked through brush toward a fairly new cabin with a gambrel roof. We had seen the cabin from the river just before we landed. Once through the brush, we continued into the grassy area surrounding the cabin. Mosquitoes attacked us from the time we left the beach, and we put on our head nets to minimize the onslaught. The right side of the cabin was incomplete. At one time Tyvek sheeting had covered that side, but now it was shredded. Inside was a small McPherson wall tent containing a bed, several chairs, and a woodstove. Outside the tent was a Coleman gas stove. The tent looked like it had been torn but was now patched. We speculated that all the damage had been caused by a marauding bear.

While doing research for this book, I read that this cabin at the Travaillant River was built by Maurine Clark, an artist from Tsiigehtchic and the granddaughter of Billy Clark, who built and operated the old trading post. She intended that the cabin be used by family members, travelers, and local hunters. Although the cabin was available to us, even if we had arrived when we were ready to spend the night, we would not have chosen to stay due to the mosquitoes, which became more prevalent and more aggressive the longer we stayed. It was the worst mosquito-infested area we had experienced since our long night of paddling on Mills Lake.

We quickly returned to the beach where Phil and Don were stretched out, enjoying the sunny afternoon. Unfortunately for them, we brought hundreds of mosquitoes with us, resulting in a fierce rebuke. I lay down on the beach for a few minutes with my back and head on my life jacket, covered with Jungle Juice on all my exposed skin and with my head net still on. Those little pests were determined to have some of my blood. When I got up a few minutes later, my life jacket was covered with dead mosquitoes, squished between my back and the life jacket.

Phil and Don quickly headed for their canoe, still complaining about the mosquitoes we had brought with us to the beach. They pushed off, Dan and I close behind. Several miles down the river, we still had quite a few mosquitoes with us.

At about 3:30 p.m., 11 mi (18 km) past Travaillant River, between a long, narrow island and the right bank of the Mackenzie, we found a gravel beach with several sandy patches that looked suitable for our camp. We began our routine of unstrapping our gear from the canoes and carrying everything to the sandy area to begin pitching tents. An hour later, the individual tents and the Tundra tent were up and ready. The weather had been almost perfect, with sunshine most of the day and a slight breeze at our backs.

31.7 mi (51.0 km) traveled today – 751 mi (1208.6 km) overall

Campsite location: N67°23'7.93" W131°48'52.3"

TWENTY-FIVE
Fatigue

"Endurance is patience concentrated." – Thomas Carlyle (Scottish historian, writer, and philosopher)

Sunday, July 9, 2006 – 10 mi (15.1 km) Past Travaillant River to 3 Miles (4.8 km) Past Adam Cabin Creek

My watch alarm went off at 6:00 a.m. A fair wind was blowing up the river, and the sun was shining through clear skies. To the southwest, clouds were forming on the horizon, and we hoped that was where they would stay. As a result of the wind and sunshine, our tents were dry.

I found it amazing how much more my tent and the Tundra tent weighed when they were wet. The tents, my Thermarest mattress, my sleeping bag, and fleece liner all went into a large red dry bag. I learned an important lesson early on to put the wet tents into plastic bags, so they wouldn't soak the rest of the gear. Climbing into a wet sleeping bag after a long day's paddle is not a pleasant experience.

Phil started our gas stove for coffee, and I heated water for oatmeal. We ate a quick breakfast, broke camp, and then quickly packed the canoes. We left at about 8:00 a.m. and paddled along the right side of the river. The river was straight and wide, flowing west and slightly south from our campsite. Many sandbars were in the area—some indicated on the map and some not. The river changes from year to year, and sandbars appear as the river subsides.

PERSEVERANCE

Dan watched ahead, looking for evidence of shallows and trying to detect the deepest, fastest-moving water. Since we couldn't see more than a couple of inches into the water, we looked for anomalies on the surface as indicators. Dan is very good at this, but occasionally our paddles hit submerged sand or gravel bars, which required quick thinking and a little luck to keep from running aground.

Several times during the morning, our paddles hit bottom, and more than once we had to climb out and pull our canoe into deeper water. Behind us, Phil and Don took advantage of our misfortune, taking different tacks and avoiding the shallows. As a result, they gained distance on us and remained close throughout the morning.

We carried a limited amount of water due to space and weight. We were getting low and were looking carefully along the shore for any sign of a stream coming into the river. One of the most obvious signs is a cut in the bank where the stream has eroded it into a small gap. Sometimes water flows over the bank without any erosion. These streams are not so obvious unless there is a large quantity of water flowing. At other times the sun reflects off the stream, and a bright glitter is the clue that leads to running water.

We spotted a cut in the bank on our right. Phil and Don were parallel to us but closer to the shore, so they paddled in to look but found a dry streambed. About 18 mi (29 km) downriver from our camp, we spotted another cut in the bank. Dan brought out his binoculars but couldn't see water. We paddled a little closer and heard the sound of water bubbling over rocks, so we continued to shore and found a stream about 3 ft (0.9 m) wide with clear, clean water flowing over the beach and into the river. The stream was the color of tea, like most streams flowing into the Mackenzie, but was free of silt.

Pulling ashore, I unpacked my pump and began filling Phil's collapsible 2.5-g (9.5-l) container. Don unpacked his pump and began filling water bottles. While we were pumping water, Phil filled his sun shower directly from the stream. When he finished, he tied the sun shower to the top of the gear in his canoe, and we pushed off the beach into the current. With clear skies throughout the day, we would be able to take warm showers in the evening.

The weather remained excellent throughout the day with the wind at our backs varying from mild to strong. After six hours of paddling, we began looking for a campsite. The right side of the river seemed to have the best beaches, so we stayed right. At 4:20 p.m. we landed on a beach similar to the beach at our last camp. It took us about an hour and a half to set up our tents and lay out our mattresses and sleeping bags.

Under the Tundra tent, we unfolded our camp chairs and relaxed. I was beginning to feel some fatigue from the long expedition. Three full weeks of paddling, all but one day when we rested in Norman Wells, and I was feeling the effects. The piercing pain in my neck continued, beginning within the first fifteen minutes of paddling each day and continuing until an hour or so after stopping. It had expanded below my neck and into my back. I didn't know what was causing the pain, but knowing I would have relief each evening and through the night kept me going during the day. I could handle one more week of it.

35.9 mi (57.8 km) traveled today – 786.9 mi (1266.4 km) overall

Campsite location: N67°13'9.2" W133°2'8.3"

TWENTY-SIX
Tsiigehtchic

"To me, there is nothing more soothing than the song of a mosquito that can't get through the mesh to bite you." – Madison Smartt Bell (American novelist)

Monday, July 10, 2006 – 3 Miles (4.8 km) Past Adam Cabin Creek to 10 Miles (16.1 km) Past Tsiigehtchic (Arctic Red River)

It was a calm morning with clear skies when we began to stir around 6:00 a.m. As I was eating breakfast, I looked out over the river at the far shore, about 2 mi (3.2 km) away. It was much different there than where we began our journey. In the middle of June when we departed Fort Providence, the melted snow and ice had swollen the river to such an extent that the beaches were flooded, and the banks were being ravaged by the strong currents, combining the soil and water to create a thick light-brown stew. Now, two and a half weeks later, the water level had fallen several feet, and rocky beaches were the norm, exposing a growing collection of beautiful sedimentary specimens for us to store in our canoes.

As the second-largest river in North America, the Mackenzie carries an enormous amount of water into the Beaufort Sea, an annual average of 340,000 cubic ft (9,628 cubic m) per second and over 529,000 cubic ft (15,000 cubic m) per second in the summer.

Although the river level was dropping, the amount of water propelled by gravity northward was massive, and the speed at which it moved was quite rapid.

In that section of the river, we saw fewer gravel bars and islands. However, it continued to take a certain amount of skill to find the fastest part of the river to paddle. The shortest distance was not always the fastest route to the destination.

At 10:00 a.m. we reached the Lower Ramparts, an 8-mi (12.9-km) section where the river narrowed to about half a mile. The Lower Ramparts weren't as spectacular as the Upper Ramparts we had traversed five days earlier. The steep canyon walls of the Lower Ramparts reached a height of approximately 300 ft (about 90 m) and consisted mainly of shale. The beaches along the shore were steep, and slabs of shale covered the shoreline. The river made an 8-mi (12.9 km) sweep, flowing northwest and curving to the southwest to the village of Tsiigehtchic where the Arctic Red River empties into the Mackenzie.

We stopped for lunch along the north shore where a small stream cascaded down the cliff and then twisted along the beach and into the river. We could hear the engines of the ferry crossing the river at Tsiigehtchick on the Dempster Highway, but it was not yet visible. Back on the river, we soon spotted the ferry as it was returning to the village.

We arrived at Tsiigehtchic at 1:30 p.m. The shoreline was muddy, and our boots sank five to 6 in (15 cm) into the ooze. Walking alongside the canoes as we pulled them up the shore was difficult. We struck up a conversation with a Gwich'in man who was putting his boat in the river. He said he was on his way to feed his dogs at his cabin downriver. He told us there was no longer a store in the village, so we were disappointed that we wouldn't be able to buy Coca-Cola for the paddle to Inuvik. We also learned there was a phone at the band office that we could use to call the RCMP and our families.

Phil and Don made the first trip into the village to make calls while Dan and I watched our canoes and gear.

The ferry at Tsiigehtchic is the northernmost ferry route in all of North America. The ferry, the MV Louis Cardinal, *was built in 1972 and operates while the river is free of ice. In the winter months, cars and trucks are able to cross the frozen river over several feet of ice.*

The Dempster Highway proceeds north and follows a path on the west side of the Arctic Red River to Tsiigehtchic. The village is east of the highway and to arrive there, you must cross the Arctic Red River. There is no bridge to Tsiigehtchic, so travelers need to make a special request for the MV Louis Cardinal *to take them across the Arctic Red River to the village before crossing the Mackenzie.*

PERSEVERANCE

Tsiigehtchic is built on high ground, and the Church of the Holy Name of Mary was the most dominate feature as we looked up from the beach. The white Roman Catholic Church with green trim was built in the late 1920s. Next to the church was the Anglican Church, also painted white with green trim. To the left we saw several buildings, including a large two-story building that we assumed was the band office.

The Gwich'in are the people of the Gwich'in Nation who live north of the Arctic Circle in fifteen communities within northeast Alaska, the northern Yukon Territory, and the Northwest Territories. It is believed they have occupied these areas for up to 20,000 years. The Gwich'in living in and around Tsiigehtchic have fished at the mouth of the Arctic Red River for centuries. In the summers, they paddle their canoes up the Arctic Red River as far as they can, then walk farther to the fishing grounds. They bring their fish down to the lowland area between Tsiigehtchic and the Mackenzie River to place them on racks for drying. In the winter, they hunt caribou, which they preserve by smoking, so they last through the year. To this day the Gwich'in still set their nets in the river and hunt caribou in the fall like their ancestors.

Dan and I watched the ferry cross from the north side of the river and land, so the vehicles could proceed up the hill on the Dempster Highway toward Fort McPherson and eventually to the Klondike Highway some 40 mi (64 km) south of Dawson City. Once the northbound vehicles were loaded, the ferry crossed the Arctic Red River and landed just below Tsiigehtchic. From our position, we couldn't see the ferry land, but it soon left the village and crossed to the landing on the north side of the Mackenzie.

A young boy went out in his boat to check his nets and came back with one whitefish and one coney. The coney is known as the sheefish in Alaska. He said he wouldn't be able to eat them because they had drowned, but he would feed them to his dogs.

When Phil and Don returned to the beach, they told us they had spoken to a local man who said he would sell us some smoked whitefish. They had made their calls home at the band office but said the people there didn't seem particularly happy to share their phone. Dan and I walked up a dirt road and found the band office and weren't greeted with much enthusiasm either. I explained that our calls would be made with calling cards, and they wouldn't have to pay, but that didn't seem to make them any happier. They asked us to keep the calls short because it was their business phone. I called Sue first and kept my call to about ten minutes. Dan called next, and when he was finished, we thanked them, sharing our appreciation for their generosity in allowing us to use their phone. I thought this might bring a smile and a "you're welcome," but all we got was a grunt or two. Regardless, we were appreciative, because they could have denied our request.

We worked our way down from the band office toward the beach and saw Phil talking to the man about the smoked fish. As it turned out, we weren't able to buy the fish, so we walked back to the canoes and left Tsiigehtchic behind at about 3:30 p.m.

We paddled for 10 more miles (16 km) before we decided to land on the right side of the river to make camp for the night. The weather throughout the day had been clear, calm, and warm. There wasn't a breath of wind at the site, and the river was so calm it reflected the mountains to the west. It looked more like a lake than a river. The temperature increased throughout the day, and our camp was the warmest it had been since we crossed the Arctic Circle.

We were camped less than 6 mi (10 km) from Point Separation, the beginning of the Mackenzie Delta. It was the point at which Alexander Mackenzie took the middle channel that carried him to the Arctic Ocean. We would be taking a channel east toward Inuvik.

The Mackenzie Delta is a massive area of approximately 4,700 square mi (12,173 sq. km) and is approximately 50 mi (80.5 km) wide, made up of rivers, streams, interwoven channels, lakes, ponds, and islands. The delta is constantly changing as the sand and mud build up into islands and change the course of the streams. The delta has three main channels. Peel Channel is the most westerly channel and connects with the Peel River, one of the routes followed by Klondike stampeders misled by Edmonton businessmen who told them it was the easiest route to the goldfields. The Middle Channel is the major conduit of water from the Mackenzie River and the widest of the three. The East Channel, the route we would be taking, flows through the town of Inuvik along the eastern edge of the Delta. All courses are navigable, but the eastern course is the shortest route to Tuktoyaktuk.

I was feeling some nervousness about our trip through the delta, not sure how obvious our route would be when we had to make decisions on which fork of the river to take.

PERSEVERANCE

Alexander Mackenzie was forced into making a decision about which route to take, as he wrote in his journal, "We were much at a loss what Channel out of some hundreds to take.. . . . I determined on taking the middle as it was a large piece of water and running N. & S." With the help of the "Eskmeaux," Mackenzie was able to reach the sea, but others long after Mackenzie's expedition weren't as fortunate. There are stories of river travelers who became confused over the abundance of choices and selected watercourses that brought them back to where they had previously been or were caught in a maze of estuaries and unable to find a way out.

After dinner and an examination of my maps of the delta region, I climbed into my tent and zapped a few dozen mosquitoes. I lay on top of my sleeping bag in my undershorts and read for an hour or so. Eventually, I fell asleep, but didn't go into my sleeping bag until the middle of the night when it was slightly cooler.

40.8 Miles (65.7 km) traveled today – 827.7 mi (1332.1 km) overall

Campsite location: N67°34'6.9" W133°57'8.1"

TWENTY-SEVEN
Jackfish Creek Cabin

"Anyone who thinks that they are too small to make a difference has never tried to fall asleep with a mosquito in the room." – Christine Todd Whitman (politician and writer)

Tuesday, July 11, 2006 – 10 Miles (16.1 km) Past Tsiigehtchic (Arctic Red River) to Jackfish Creek

I woke up at 4:00 a.m. thinking about my granddaughter, Caitlyn, who was less than two months old. In my call to Sue from Tsiigehtchic, I learned that doctors had just completed a hearing test on her, because they suspected she may have little or no hearing. Sue did not have the results yet, and I worried about how Caitlyn's life might be without the ability to hear. I had learned firsthand of the difficulties deaf children have socializing with others when my school was the site of a program for deaf children. There is a difference of opinion as to whether blindness or deafness is a greater disability. The teacher of the class of deaf students told me she thought deafness was a far greater disability because so much of development is learned through the spoken word. The challenge for parents and children alike in either case is frightening.

Caitlyn was born on May 22 in Bellingham, WA. Her father, our son, Reed, had just been selected as the head football coach of Squalicum High School, and he was in the process of putting together a spring program while still teaching at Arlington High School in Arlington, WA. Caitlyn's mother, Lisa, was teaching at an elementary school near Burlington, WA, and was expecting to complete the school year before the baby was born. Caitlyn was about one month premature, but her weight and length were in the average range.

I was in Longview, WA, serving as a school improvement facilitator at St. Helens Elementary School when I got the call that Lisa was on the way to the hospital. I left immediately, and during my four hour drive, Sue called to say that Caitlyn had been born, and she and Lisa were doing well.

When I arrived in Lisa's hospital room, I found Sue, Lisa, Reed, and Lisa's parents looking worried. They told me that an hour or so after Caitlyn was born, her breathing became labored, and she began turning blue. Caitlyn was being stabilized and would be flown by helicopter to Seattle Children's Hospital. Prior to being loaded onto the helicopter, they wheeled her into Lisa's room inside a plastic box with tubes feeding her oxygen to keep her alive.

Reed and I drove to Seattle and arrived at the hospital late that night. My other son, John, had driven from Port Orchard, WA, and my daughter, Melissa, had driven from Mount Vernon, WA, to Seattle to support Reed, Lisa, and Caitlyn.

Caitlyn spent two weeks at Seattle Children's Hospital and one and one half weeks at Providence Medical Center in Everett, WA. I was able to visit her several times at the hospitals during that period. When I left on our Mackenzie trip, she was making good progress, but we worried there might be long-term effects as a result of her premature birth.

At 6:00 a.m. I got up, stuffed my sleeping bag, fleece liner, and Thermarest into their bags, and took down my tent. Life on an expedition is a set of routines: set up, take down, paddle, rest, pump water, and more. I had enjoyed every element of the trip, but I was looking forward to the end.

By 8:00 a.m., Phil and Don were on the water. They left as soon as the Tundra tent was down while Dan and I stowed it in the canoe, lashed down our gear, and then positioned the spray skirt over the top and secured it to the canoe.

Once we left the beach, Phil and Don were nearly out of sight. This had been the pattern over the past week or two. By the first rest stop, we would either catch up or pass them. I wasn't sure why we were moving faster. We seemed to be carrying at least as much weight as they were. They were older but very fit. Dan's strength was probably a major factor in our speed, but I matched him stroke for stroke nearly all the time, so I believed I was doing my part. Regardless, I thought it helped Phil and Don's motivation to lead the way at least some of the time.

We reached Separation Point earlier than expected, so we were making good time. The river was still moving swiftly, but it would soon be spreading out into hundreds of branches, and we knew the swiftness would diminish. We stayed to the right of a long island. Just beyond it we knew the East Channel would separate from the main channel. We stopped for a short rest along a muddy beach and then continued on.

I estimated we would see the East Channel about an hour after the rest stop, but it appeared in half that time. Our goal for the day was to reach the NWT Wildlife cabin that Keith Hickling had located on our map back in Norman Wells. We weren't sure about the size and shape of the cabin but hoped it would accommodate us overnight.

The East Channel was quite narrow, with numerous small, stagnant estuaries branching out from either side. It was difficult to determine if the streams were flowing into the channel, out of the channel, or were just sloughs with no water movement at all. There was very little current in the channel, and the only ripples on the surface came from occasional gusts of wind. We were surprised it was so hot that far north and would have liked to shed some layers of clothing, but we had to keep our skin covered to protect us from the mosquitoes.

After stopping for lunch, we continued on, following the map very closely because we didn't want to miss Jackfish Creek and the Wildlife cabin. We expected Jackfish Creek to be larger than most of the narrow channels we were passing and were relying on Keith's description.

As we passed a low muddy island on our right, we were attacked from the air by a pair of Arctic terns. They squawked and soared above us, then dove toward our heads. I watched one come within an inch of Dan's head and then turn quickly and make another dive just as close. Without a doubt, they had a nest nearby and were giving us a stern warning that this was their territory, and they weren't willing to share. Once we passed the island, they seemed satisfied and returned to shore.

To our left was the widest estuary we had seen coming into the East Channel since we had left the main channel. Soon afterward we found Jackfish Creek just as Keith had described. We took a sharp hairpin turn to the right to enter the creek, which was flowing at an angle into the East Channel. Keith had told us the cabin was about 200 ft (61 m) up the creek, but after paddling more than 500 ft (152 m), we still hadn't seen it. Jackfish Creek was very still, and we didn't seem to be paddling against any current. After a long straight stretch, the creek

PERSEVERANCE

swung to the left, and just into the turn we saw a path leading up to the cabin, almost half a mile from the East Channel.

Dan and I landed along the bank at the base of the path and kept the canoe parallel to the shore. I stepped out, and my boot sank nearly a foot into the mud. I stretched my other leg out to step closer to the bank, hoping for solid ground. Unfortunately, my other foot sank in just as deep. With my feet apart, I couldn't get either boot out of the mud. Dan climbed out and tried to help me, but his boots also sank into the mud. After several minutes of struggling, we helped each other to more secure ground. Phil and Don saw our predicament and were able to find a more secure landing spot.

We walked up the path and found the front door of the cabin was locked. We went to the back and found the back door was unlocked, as Keith had assured us it would be. However, several iron bars were nailed across the doorway for protection from bears, and we had to remove the bars to enter. Inside were two sofas, two tables, several chairs, a woodstove for heat, a propane stove for cooking, shelves, and cabinets stocked with cooking utensils, plates, bowls, cups, spices, paper towels, and a limited amount of dried food. In a separate room were eight bunks. It looked like a grand place to stay.

Our next project was to unload our gear from the canoe and bring it to the cabin. The more we walked through the mud, the worse it became. We were eventually able to get what we needed to the cabin, so we could relax during the remainder of the afternoon and evening.

At 8:00 p.m. I couldn't wait any longer to find out the results of Caitlyn's hearing evaluation. I called Sue on the satellite phone. The news couldn't have been better; Caitlyn had full hearing in both ears. Sue asked me how I was doing because I sounded exhausted. I told her I was tired but otherwise doing well. With the good news about Caitlyn, I went to bed confident I would be able to sleep.

Sometimes what seems to be a good thing turns out to be anything but. It was a blessing to be out of the weather, to cook our dinner on a propane stove, to sit at a table to eat, and to relax on a sofa. However, I probably should have pitched my tent outside because that night in the cabin was anything but a blessing. It was extremely hot, and I knew I would sweat profusely inside my sleeping bag. I lay on top of the bunkbed in my undershorts, sweating anyway. I finally fell asleep, but at around 2:00 a.m., I was attacked by mosquitoes. Dan woke up at the same time, and we both got up and checked the doors and windows to see if we could find out where they were getting in. Everything was closed or screened, so I guessed they must have been inside and came alive when fresh blood was available. I used the mosquito zapper and killed hundreds, but they kept coming. I couldn't get into my sleeping bag because of the heat, which meant exposing myself to these predators. I lathered up with Jungle Juice, which kept them from biting. However, the buzzing was driving me crazy. My anticipation of a good night's sleep didn't become a reality.

38.5 mi (62.0 km) traveled today – 866.2 mi (1394.1 km) overall

Cabin location: N67°57'57.9" W134°00'57.1

"When you prepare for something big in your life and work towards it with such intensity, it takes confidence to take a day off and have peace with it." – J.R. Rim (Canadian author)

Wednesday, July 12, 2006

We were up by 8:30 a.m. and decided to spend a second day at the cabin and do some fishing in Jackfish Creek. The water was muddy, but we hoped to catch a northern pike or a few walleye for dinner. Keith Hickling said there were also grayling and whitefish in the creek. We had failed to catch walleye in some of the tributaries of the Mackenzie earlier in the trip, so we hoped to have some success there.

Dan and I walked down to the canoe at about 9:45 a.m., pulled out our fishing tackle, and rigged our poles for walleye. We paddled down to where Jackfish Creek flowed into the East Channel, hoping to catch a fish in the back eddies there, but we had no success. We paddled back up the creek and past the cabin but still had no luck. I continued paddling farther up the creek while Dan fished from the bow. If there were fish in the creek, they weren't interested in our lures.

There was very little accessible shoreline near the cabin, and as we paddled farther upstream, the shoreline became even less accessible. Fishing from shore would be impossible. Scrubby green alder and arctic willow covered the landscape, interspersed with tall black spruce trees, often in groups of half a dozen or more. Through the bushes we saw purple wildflowers that we suspected were wild sweet peas. Bushes hung out over the water, and we saw several spruce trees leaning over the creek, their root systems exposed where the bank had caved away.

We found a narrow stream coming into the creek and decided to see if there might be better fishing away from Jackfish Creek. I didn't expect to paddle very far, because the alder, willow, and spruce trees hanging over the stream looked like they would soon block our way. However, instead of a blockage, the steam turned sharply to the left, and we could see a long distance ahead. I kept paddling as Dan threw his lure out into the muddy water. Again, he could not entice a single fish. Either there were no fish in the stream, or they weren't interested in the lures he was using.

We paddled back to Jackfish Creek and continued farther up, stopping at several streams to fish, with the same result. When we found grass growing in the water in large patches, we paddled close, looking for the kind of movement we had seen just beyond Mills Lake where we caught the big northern pike. Nothing moved, and the few casts we made were fruitless. We continued on and found another stream of moderately clear coffee-colored water. The stream was larger than the others, so we paddled several hundred yards using the lures recommended to us for catching walleye. Unfortunately, our fishing expedition was a bust, so we decided to pump about 3 g (11.4 l) of water to replenish our dwindling supply back at the cabin.

It was getting close to lunchtime, so we began our 3-mi (5-km) paddle back, arriving at the cabin around 1:00 p.m. We spent the remainder of the afternoon relaxing, trying to regain some strength and enthusiasm for our last paddle before Inuvik. I also made a careful search to see if I could find where the mosquitoes were entering the cabin. I discovered a stove pipe in the ceiling near where we were sleeping. When I looked up through the pipe, I could see blue sky. I expected that was the conduit for the previous night's invasion. I crumpled up some newspapers and stuffed them in the pipe. Then I placed a couple of strips of tape across the bottom of the pipe to keep the newspapers from falling out or being blown out by a gust of wind.

We were determined not to spend another miserable night in the cabin with the company of mosquitoes. After dinner and before I went to bed, I stretched the mosquito net from one side of the Tundra tent across the open door at the back of the cabin. My strategy was to not only stop the invading mosquitos but also to let in fresh air to keep the temperature down to a reasonable level. We also lit mosquito coils, filling the inside of the cabin with the sweet smelling smoke that the little pests detested.

Our second night at the cabin was far different from our first. We were able to zap nearly all the mosquitos in the cabin, and the further precautions worked, and we were able to sleep comfortably until morning

Cabin location: N67°57'57.9" W134°00'57.1

TWENTY-EIGHT
To Inuvik

"One part at a time, one day at a time, we can accomplish any goal we set for ourselves." – Karen Casey (American author and public speaker)

Thursday, July 13, 2006 – Jackfish Creek Cabin to Inuvik

I had set the alarm for 4:30 a.m., so we could get a good start and be able to reach the Inuvik NCTL office before it closed. I assumed they would close at 4:00 p.m., as in Norman Wells and Hay River. We needed an early start and a strong paddle in order to get the truck keys from the office, load the canoes and gear, and find a spot at the campground.

Phil put a pot of water on the propane stove while we stuffed our sleeping bags and rolled up our mattresses. Our breakfast was the same as every morning (with the exception of the pancake breakfast in Norman Wells): instant oatmeal and breakfast bars. The cabin needed some cleaning after our two-day occupation, so we washed the dishes, swept the floor, and put everything we had moved back in place. I made sure the newspaper I had stuffed in the chimney hung down, so it was clearly visible. I didn't want our generous friends from the wildlife department to get smoked out or have a chimney fire if they hooked up a woodstove and lit a fire without removing the newspaper.

We carried our gear from the cabin and set it down on the grassy bank just above the creek. We went back to make our final inspection of the cabin and to secure the back door. After a stop at the outhouse, we walked down the trail, ready to face the muddy task of loading the canoes.

The mud was worse than when we arrived because of our earlier escapades, so I went down alongside our canoe while Dan handed down the gear. I was soon stuck and had to move the canoe backwards and forwards to gain full access to it since I couldn't move my feet. Phil and Don used the same procedure, and it wasn't long before the canoes were loaded and ready for us to climb aboard. This last step wasn't so easy. Dan was able to stretch his legs far enough to reach the canoe and avoid the deepest mud, but I couldn't lift my boots out of the mud. I tried to twist my feet and pull them free, but they wouldn't budge. Eventually, I pulled my left foot out of the boot and stepped into the canoe. I did the same with the right foot and then began the task of retrieving my boots. I leaned out of the canoe and scooped out handfuls of mud from alongside the boots until I could free them from the mud. I washed off the muck, put the boots back on, and we were on our way.

During the process of leaving, the mosquitoes attacked us with a vengeance, trying to get their fill of our blood before we left the area. Jungle Juice is the best insect repellent I have found, and with a formula that includes 98 percent Deet, it kept the pests from landing for more than a fraction of a second on exposed skin.

At 5:30 a.m. we pushed away from shore and paddled one mile down Jackfish Creek and back onto the East Channel. The mosquitoes stayed with us, refusing to give up. I have read about moose being driven mad by these pests, crashing through the brush and charging into lakes and rivers for protection. Fortunately for us, the Jungle Juice did its job, and we were able to carry on with a minimum of annoyance. The mosquitoes stayed with us well into our first break, which was on a muddy bank with a log to sit on.

The Mackenzie Delta was formed by silt from the river, deposited as the river slowed when reaching the ocean. Over centuries these deposits created land stretching for miles into what was once the Arctic Ocean. Environment Canada has determined that over 141,000,000 tons (128,000,000 tonnes) of sediment are deposited in the delta each year, almost all of it from May to October. About 17 percent comes from the Peel River. The remaining amount comes from the Mackenzie and its tributaries. The Liard River provides the largest contribution of sediment to the Mackenzie.

Between our first and second breaks, more Arctic terns screeched warnings for us to stay away from their nesting areas. The muddy banks didn't look like

PERSEVERANCE

good spots to stop anyway, but I didn't think the terns would understand if I shouted that fact to them.

When it was time for the second stop, we began looking for a beach without mud. The river channel twisted and turned, and several likely spots turned out to be just more muddy shorelines. After several attempted landings, we came across a small hillside with an outcropping of shale. This was the first solid footing along the shore of the East Channel we had seen in the past two days. We kept our break to a minimum, so we would stay on schedule. I checked the map for the distance we had traveled since leaving the cabin and was doubtful we could reach Inuvik in time if we didn't pick up our pace. After discussing this with Dan, we told Phil and Don that we were going to dig in and try to make up some time. We would see them in Inuvik.

The river was very still, and we observed almost no current in some areas and only moderate current in others. I was certain the river was not going to help us along, so we paddled harder and deeper. I watched the map closely because several channels were coming in and leaving the East Channel. Eventually, we saw a few cabins and suspected we were getting closer to Inuvik. The structures weren't occupied, and we assumed they were hunting or fishing cabins.

When we were within 7 mi (11 km) of Inuvik, a 14-ft (4.3 m) aluminum boat loaded with furniture passed us, heading up the channel. It was the first boat we had seen since we left Tsiigehtchic (Arctic Red River). At 3:00 p.m. we saw the first buildings in Inuvik. Because we had changed the time on our watches, we weren't going to have the same debacle we had in Norman Wells.

At 3:20 p.m. we passed the 160-foot (48.8-meter) Coast Guard boat *Dumit* tied to a pier. Soon after that we passed a houseboat moored to shore and asked a woman on the deck if we were close to the NTCL dock and offices. She told us we had about 3 mi (5 km) to paddle. We dug in again, determined to reach NTCL by 4:00 p.m.

At 3:45 p.m. we arrived at the NTCL building and found a spot to land along the shoreline. Dan secured the canoe as I climbed the bank. I was pleased to see my Ford F-250 about 100 ft (30.5 m) away.

I ran to the office and saw their hours posted on a window. All that rushing was unnecessary because I discovered they would be open until 5:00 p.m. I signed some papers and was given the keys to the truck.

When I returned to the river, I saw that Dan had found a spot to unload our canoe, away from the muddy bank. A metal grate about 15 ft (4.6 m) wide and

25 ft (7.6 m) long stretched out into the river, making for an excellent landing. I walked over to the truck and was relieved when it started right up. I drove to the landing, backed the truck close to the grate, and climbed out just as Phil and Don arrived. We removed our gear from the canoes and loaded it into the truck. Then we sponged down the canoes to remove the muddy film and loaded them on the rack above the canopy. After lashing them down, we drove into town and stopped at a store to ask where the RCMP office was located.

When we arrived there, we made what turned out to be our final report. We asked about options for getting our canoe back if Dan and I paddled to Tuktoyaktuk. The officer explained that our options were limited unless we were willing to spend more than the canoe was worth. Fuel alone would be about $800 for a boat—if we could find one to make the trip. Another option was to have the canoe airlifted, but that would be even more expensive. He made it clear that prices in Inuvik were very high, because it was so remote, and prices would be even higher in Tuk. There was also the time constraint. We weren't sure we could get the canoe back to Inuvik before we needed to begin our drive home.

It was apparent that we had two options: paddle down to Tuk, try to sell the canoe, and fly back to Inuvik or make Inuvik our last stop. Reluctantly, we decided not to paddle to Tuk. We went to the Happy Valley Territorial Campground overlooking the river, set up our tents, and then drove into town.

Two structures there stood out for their uniqueness and size: Sir Alexander Mackenzie School and the igloo-shaped Our Lady of Victory Church. This Catholic church was constructed in the late 1950s and opened in 1960.

We stopped at the Eskimo Inn for dinner. Dan and I ordered musk ox burgers, which tasted okay, and Phil and Don ordered bison burgers which they said were delicious. We met a woman there who told us we should stop by Alexander Mackenzie School. We weren't sure what we would see there, but we accepted her advice.

The school appeared to be the largest structure in Inuvik, a massive two-story building set on a knoll in the center of town. A large banner hanging near the entrance declared, "Let the Healing Begin." We walked inside and saw a gathering of Aboriginal men, women, and children—I estimated to be nearly 1,000. Many were chanting and dancing to the rhythm of several drums. I asked a man and his wife to explain the significance of the event and learned it was a reunion of those who had attended that residential school. The gentleman said the people were taken from their homes, their cultures, and their communities and forced to attend the school to "westernize" them. He spoke in a soft voice, not angry but expressing sorrow in what they had each experienced. He explained this was the first reunion, but there would likely be more.

Inuvik is a relatively new city, established in 1954 to resettle inhabitants of Aklavik, a village located in the middle of the Mackenzie Delta. It was believed that the changes in the different river channels would soon wipe out Aklavik. As it turned out, the "doomed" village survived and maintains a population of approximately 600 inhabitants. Following this move, Inuvik became the center for the regional government and remains so to this day.

Sir Alexander Mackenzie School opened in 1959 and housed Inuit, First Nations, and Metis students from villages throughout the region. It was also the school for many Caucasian students living in and around Inuvik.

The Indian residential schools, including Sir Alexander Mackenzie School, were government-funded, church-run schools with the purpose of eliminating parental involvement in the spiritual, cultural, and intellectual development of Aboriginal children. A Catholic dormitory and an Anglican dormitory were managed by priests and others hired to supervise the Aboriginal children. Many of the residential schools have a dark past in which physical and sexual abuse occurred and was often covered up by those in charge. More than thirty victims of sexual abuse at the Inuvik school came forward, and eventually, four men who worked in the dorms were convicted of sexual abuse and spent time in prison. Unfortunately, when the trials took place and names were exposed, four of the abused boys, who were then grown men, committed suicide.

More than 150,000 Aboriginal children were taken from their homes throughout Canada and placed in 130 residential schools beginning in the late 1870s. The last residential school closed in 1996. Many of these schools did not allow the children to speak their native language or engage in any of their culture while attending there. In 1998 the federal government of Canada issued a statement of reconciliation admitting that students had suffered abuses at the schools. A multi-million dollar compensation fund was established for those who had suffered by being removed from their homes and placed in residential schools. In May 2006, all parties agreed to the largest settlement in Canadian history. The settlement funded a truth and reconciliation commission that would provide opportunities for individuals, families, and communities to share their experiences and to raise public awareness of the residential schools—a sad part of Canadian history they hoped would never be forgotten. Several national events sponsored by the truth and reconciliation commission were held from 2010 through 2014. The second event held in Inuvik was from June 28 through July 1, 2011.

"From 1958, when it first opened, until 1979, there was never a year in which Grollier Hall in Inuvik did not employ at least one dormitory supervisor who would later be convicted for sexually abusing students." – from the truth and reconciliation commission's final report

After the Sir Alexander Mackenzie Residential School closed, the building was used as a community elementary school until it closed in 2012. In 2014, the building was demolished.

We stood at the open door of the school, listening to the drummers and watching the dancers step to the rhythm while others stood near us in quiet conversation. After about an hour, we returned to the truck and drove back to the campground where we discussed how difficult it must have been for the children to be taken from their homes, placed in a strange environment, and separated from their families and their communities.

I only hope a lesson can be learned from this failed experiment, and an end will come to the horrific events in other parts of the world where ethnic and cultural atrocities continue to this day.

It took me a long time to fall asleep as I thought about the many victims in the United States (Aboriginals, African slaves, and others) whose lives were forever altered because of the white man's sense of superiority. The event we attended was a sad, sober reminder of the past, but we felt honored to have attended.

38.9 mi (62.6 km) traveled today – 905.1 mi (1456.7 km) overall

NTCL Landing, Inuvik N68°22'34.9" W133°46'18.2"

TWENTY-NINE
Exploring Inuvik

The best way to look back at life fondly is to meet it—and those along your journey—warmly, kindly and mindfully." – Rasheed Ogunlaru (author and public speaker)

Friday, July 14, 2006 – Inuvik

In the campground, platforms were built for tent campers to erect their tents on a flat surface above the ground. Our platform was large enough for all three tents if we squeezed them together. The campground also had showers and laundry facilities.

As soon as I awakened at around 7:00 a.m., I headed for the showers. I don't think I've ever enjoyed a shower as much as that one. After breakfast we all climbed into the truck and headed to town to buy laundry detergent. We stopped by the town office for information about Inuvik and sites to see in and around the town. We learned that an art fair was opening that night and would open again at noon the next day. We would have the opportunity to purchase paintings, sculptures, crafts, and more, if interested. We were told there would be a great deal of Aboriginal art available. When Sue and I lived in Alaska, we admired Aboriginal art, particularly art created by the Inuit. We were able to purchase a few pieces at that time, but Sue was attending the University of Alaska, and I was a beginning teacher, which meant we didn't have much money for such extras, so I was looking forward to this new opportunity.

At the town office, we learned about a community greenhouse not far from Sir Alexander Makenzie School, so we drove up to take a look around. The massive greenhouse had a rounded roof consisting almost entirely of windows above raised garden plots with flowers, fruit, and vegetables. From my experience in Fairbanks, I knew how fast plants grew when exposed to sunlight twenty-four hours a day, and I was sure the families with plots in the greenhouse were treated to fresh vegetables and fruit throughout the summer.

We walked upstairs and met a young woman named Jessica who had lived in Inuvik for two years after moving from Vancouver Island in British Columbia. She had an archeology degree and had come to the area to meet and learn about the people of the Arctic. During the winter, she was a substitute teacher at the high school. She was concerned that the young Indigenous people were not learning the Gwich'in language. Efforts had been made to teach them the words, but they were not using the language. We told Jessica that we were planning to attend the art fair the next day, and she suggested we look at some of the Native art for sale on the third floor of the Corporation Building.

We left the community greenhouse and stopped by the Corporation Building to check out the gallery. We saw some beautiful carvings and other artwork, but the prices seemed quite expensive, so we decided to wait until the art fair the next day.

We stopped by the RCMP office and met a Mountie named George Doolittle. We had a nice chat about our trip and the people we met along the river, including Lisa McDonald, who is George's niece. He said Lisa had sent him a bear roast just the previous week.

Dan and I were lamenting that we weren't able to paddle to Tuktoyaktuk, so we stopped by the information center in town to check on ways we might be able to get out to Tuk. They sent us to a tour company where we learned that for $275 we could take a half-day flight to Tuk, which included a tour when we arrived.

Before deciding on the tour, we thought we'd inquire about getting a flight without the tour for the four of us. We went to the airport and checked with Aklak Air, the local airline that flew between Inuvik and Tuk, to see if a direct flight without the tour might be less expensive. They told us we could take the regular scheduled flight for $230 but that we needed to book it through the tour company.

Back at the tour company office, they told us that information was incorrect. We decided not to keep playing this back-and-forth game and booked ourselves on a flight and tour that would leave at noon the next day. They said they would pick us up in town, take us to the airport, fly us to Tuk, take us on a tour, fly us back to the Inuvik airport, and then drive us back to town.

As we left the tour company office, we decided to take another look at the art gallery. We drove to the Corporation Building and climbed the stairs to the third floor. I purchased a sculpture made of caribou bones carved into the shape of birds with long necks for $90. As we were leaving, an artist arrived with two new pieces. One was a musk ox carved from soapstone. It was an exquisite piece. I had seen similar pieces that weren't nearly as well done for several hundred dollars in Seattle.

In the late 1960s when my wife and I were living in Fairbanks, the University of Alaska was raising musk ox for research. I visited the fenced area where the beasts were held to observe and take photos. On one of those occasions, I stuck my camera lens through the wires of a chain-link fence to take a photo of a musk ox grazing close by. Just as I snapped the photo, the animal lowered his head and charged. I jumped back just in time to avoid a serious injury. The animal left a twelve-inch bow in the fence.

Regardless of my incident in Fairbanks, I continued to be mesmerized with this beautiful creature of the Artic and for many years had wanted a sculpture of a musk ox. I was surprised and happy to purchase the sculpture for only $180.

Phil and Dan walked back to the campground as Don and I drove to the recreation center to see if we could catch a glimpse of the artwork displays being prepared for the next day. The organizers seemed frantic, cleaning the floors, so they could set up tables as the artists began coming in early. When the organizers saw us peering through the doorway and trying to get a glimpse of the operation, they asked if we would be willing to help with the setup. We saw it as a perfect opportunity to preview much of the artwork. We were able to talk to several of the artists between sweeping, mopping, setting up tables, putting up posters, helping the artists carry in their creations, running errands, and whatever else was needed. We spent a good portion of the afternoon there, working in the hall and meeting some amazing people. When we returned to the campground, we discovered that Phil and Dan had washed all of our dirty clothes.

While we were packing our clothes, Dan mentioned that he would like to get a photo of the four of us in front of the Coast Guard boat, *Dumit*. We climbed in the truck, drove down to the river, and worked our way through narrow streets and gravel roads, trying to find the spot where we had seen the boat on our paddle into town. Unfortunately, the *Dumit* had departed. We spotted the houseboat we had seen from the river where the woman had given us directions to NTCL. I knocked on the door, and the same woman answered. I asked her if she would take a picture of the four of us in front of the river. She invited us to come aboard and stand on her deck, where she took photos with each of our cameras. I asked her to stand by Dan, Phil, and Don, so I could snap a photo of her as well.

She introduced herself as Sandy Hanson and told us the history of their houseboat. She and her husband had purchased a small cabin, which they placed on a barge to create their own houseboat. It was a "512 Cabin" built in the 1950s when Inuvik was just getting started and wasn't yet called by that name. There were many of the 16 x 32 sq. ft (4.9 x 9.8 sq. m) cabins that got their name from their 512 sq. ft (156 sq. m) size. Many of the Inuit who were moved from Aklavik to Inuvik were housed in the tiny houses, sometimes with a family of eight or more people crammed inside.

Sandy and her husband took dinner cruises on their barge until the government stopped them because they didn't meet regulations. Now they used the barge for family and friends. In the fall they hunted from the barge and got a moose almost every year. She took us on a tour of the cabin, which included an upper deck and a pilot station.

Sandy's husband, Frank, was an Inuit and a civil engineer. Since laws required that companies have 51-percent Aboriginal ownership, Frank was frequently asked by many companies to be a partner in their businesses. As a result, he had become a partner in several companies in the Arctic. Sandy said she would like us to meet Frank, but he was having dinner with his brother at the time. We invited them to visit our campsite later.

Back in camp, we ate dinner and then went to the opening of the Great Northwest Art Festival. While we were looking over the artwork and talking with the new friends Don and I had met earlier, we met a young couple, Jennifer and Eric, who lived in Inuvik. Jennifer was originally from Nova Scotia but lived on Baffin Island before coming to Inuvik. Eric was a pilot for Aklak Air and was on call for the EMTs. He told us about a recent flight to Fort Good Hope to pick up a man who had been cut severely in the head by a machete. Someone had broken into the man's cabin, and when he confronted the intruder, he was attacked. When Eric arrived, the man's head was bandaged and bleeding. He and the EMTs took the patient to Inuvik even though he protested and wanted to go "south."

We also met a young woman, Katherine, from Inuvik who was originally from Quebec. She was a wildlife biologist and had attended Washington State University, where she studied cougars. We thought it was an appropriate college to study cougars since the mascot for WSU is the cougar.

When we left the art festival, we drove around to see more of the town. We passed Jennifer and Eric, out walking their dog. They waved for us to stop and invited us to a barbecue at their home the following night. It seemed that everywhere we went, we found friendly people who were eager to talk to us.

After a long and interesting day, we headed back to camp, ready for a good night's sleep.

THIRTY
Tuktoyaktuk

"In Alaska, the beaches are slumping so much, people are having to move houses. In Tuktoyaktuk, the land is starting to go under water. The glaciers are melting and the permafrost is melting. There are new species of birds and fish and insects showing up. The Arctic is a barometer for the health of the world. If you want to know how healthy the world is, come to the Arctic and feel its pulse." – Sheila Watt-Cloutier (Canadian Inuit activist)

Saturday, July 15, 2006 – Inuvik and Tuktoyaktuk

I woke up early and headed for the showers. When I returned to the camp, Dan was making pancakes. We puttered around camp for a while, and then at 10:15 a.m. we climbed into the truck for our drive to the start of our trip to Tuktoyaktuk. Unfortunately, the truck's battery was dead. This was a mystery to me because it had run fine the previous day, and the lights weren't left on. The campground manager gave me a jump-start and recommended a repair shop. We had plenty of time, so we drove to the shop and were told the repairman on duty was busy, but they would be open until 6:00 p.m. If we could come back later in the afternoon, they could work on the truck. That would work out well for us because we would return from our tour in time to be back to the shop by 4:00 p.m.

We drove to the tour office, where we were loaded into a van that took us to the airport. Our plane seated twelve passengers, so a third of the seats were filled by the four of us. We strapped ourselves in, and the plane took off, quickly making a turn north over Inuvik. From my seat, I could see the entire city, including the campground, the igloo church, Sir Alexander Mackenzie School, and the greenhouse. Inuvik is situated on the eastern edge of the Mackenzie Delta on high land. I tried to follow the East Channel, but with the plane's wing blocking much of my view, all I could see was a tangle of channels around islands and lakes. It wasn't difficult to see how easy it would be to get lost out there.

In the summer of 1972, two eleven-year-old boys and one thirteen-year-old boy forced to live in the residential school in Inuvik snuck out of Stringer Hall to smoke cigarettes that one of them had stolen from a dormitory supervisor. Worried about facing the strict supervisor after returning, they decided to run back to their homes in Tuktoyaktuk. It was not a well-planned journey, because they left with only the clothes they were wearing. One of the eleven-year-olds, Bernard Andreason, later recalled that they thought they could make it to Tuk in a day or two. Even though it would be impossible to travel 80 mi (almost 130 km) in that short time period, having to cross the jumble of streams, lakes, and islands of the Mackenzie Delta would make the trek nearly impossible for these young boys. Miraculously, Bernard survived the nearly weeklong trip but arrived in Tuk in serious condition. The other eleven-year-old was later found dead. The thirteen-year-old was never found.

Seeing the area from the airplane, it was amazing to me that any of the boys could have survived more than a day or two in that environment.

During the half-hour flight, the trees became smaller and eventually vanished. As we neared Tuk, I saw several small cone-shaped hills, called pingos, rising up from the otherwise flat tundra.

The word "pingo" is an Inuvialuit word meaning "small hill." The scientific name for pingo is "hydrolaccolith." Pingos are formed from lake beds in permafrost areas through a process of freezing and thawing of water fed by an aquafer. Sediments on the surface are pushed up by the freezing ice over hundreds of years. The center of a pingo is ice, and the surface is tundra, similar to the ground surface in the region. They can reach a height of 230 ft (70 m). They can be as wide as 1,650 ft (500 m). Just outside of Tuktoyaktuk is the Ibyuk Pingo, the second-largest pingo in the world with a width of nearly 1,000 ft (approximately 300 m) and a height of approximately 161 ft (49 m). It has been estimated to be approximately 1,300 years old and is still growing at a rate of just under 1 in (2 cm) per year. About one fourth of the world's pingos are located along the coastline near Tuktoyaktuk. The largest pingo in the world, at a height of 178 ft (54 m), is called the Kadleroshilik Pingo and is located 25 mi (40 km) southeast of Prudhoe Bay, AK.

A van was waiting for us when we landed in Tuk. As we rode toward the village, we saw several pingos rising from the flat tundra. Our driver and tour guide assured us that we would have the opportunity to climb to the top of one of them.

He drove us out to a beach on the shore of the Arctic Ocean. The water was relatively calm, with ripples and an occasional whitecap. Don, Dan, and I waded into the ocean instead of swimming, as we had considered doing. A young couple on our tour stripped down to their swimsuits and jumped in. The water was cold but not as cold as I had suspected—about the same temperature as the Puget Sound, the water I swam in as a kid. Dan, Phil, and I picked up a few rocks from the beach to add to our collections while Don shook his head in disgust.

We stopped at a concrete structure marking the end of the Trans Canada Trail. We also visited a small shop where some of the local women were sewing fur slippers, mukluks, hats, and dolls. Don purchased a pair of slippers for his wife, Sandy. We visited two small, old churches before stopping at the community freezer, where local families froze their moose, caribou, and other meats in an underground tunnel carved out of the permafrost. We weren't able to enter, but a sign out front showed a diagram of the layout: two crossing tunnels with more than twenty individual family cutouts for placing frozen food. Before we boarded our plane, we were taken to a nearby pingo and, as promised, were able to walk to the top.

When we returned to Inuvik, I couldn't start the truck, so I called a tow truck. The driver jumped the battery for $20, and we drove directly to the repair shop just as everyone was leaving. It turned out that the shop didn't close at 6:00 p.m., as we were told. Closing time on Saturday was 4:00 p.m. However, the owner took pity on us and asked one of his mechanics, an older gentleman, if he would have a look at the truck. It didn't take long for him to diagnose the problem: the alternator had died and needed to be replaced. Unfortunately, all the parts stores were closed, which meant we couldn't get a replacement until Monday. The mechanic saw the disappointment on our faces and said he would see if he could find one on a truck out back. He left us and soon returned with one he had removed from a 2000 Ford diesel truck. He began taking the

PERSEVERANCE

defective alternator out of my truck while the four of us and the owner leaned over and watched. Suddenly, the mechanic stood up and said he couldn't work with all of us hanging over watching, and he looked like he was about to leave. The owner volunteered to take Phil, Don, and Dan back to the campground, leaving me with the mechanic, who seemed satisfied and went back to work.

Once the alternator was out, the mechanic attempted to install the replacement. He had to improvise to make it fit, but once it was installed, he discovered it, too, was bad. He took it out, went back behind the garage, and returned with an alternator from a 2001 Ford diesel engine. Fortunately, that alternator worked. I paid for the repair and slipped the mechanic an extra $20 for his effort on our behalf.

In the fall of 2018, I sold my diesel pickup. The alternator from Inuvik was still on the truck and working well.

I left the repair shop with a reduced level of anxiety and returned to the campground. Phil, Dan, and Don were talking to a German man named Walter who was the driver of a bus parked in a camp spot across the road. His big red bus carried twenty-four passengers and had sleeping berths for all of them. Walter was the driver and tour guide, and he also cooked the meals for everyone. The sides of the bus below the sleeping berths opened upward to reveal a sink, food lockers, utensils, and everything else needed to prepare meals. I had seen such a bus, perhaps that very one, when I was in Alaska a few years earlier. We offered Walter a beer, and he gave us each some of his homemade potato salad.

We drove to the Great Northern Art Festival and spent a few minutes with our new friends before driving over to Eric and Jennifer's home for the barbecue. We learned that they were very adventurous and had sailed with a Norwegian adventurer trying to traverse the Northwest Passage. We also met a man named Julian who was working on the Trans Canada Trail and had done some of the canoeing with Jamie Bastedo (the man we met in Norman Wells who was leading the group of Aboriginal boys on their canoe trip down the river). Julian was a teacher at Aurora College in recreation and leadership.

We returned to camp and spent a couple hours talking to Walter, who recounted his many adventures in the Arctic. He invited us for breakfast the following morning before we departed Inuvik.

John R. Richardson

The sun setting over the river at our camp

Phil and Don along the shore of the Lower Ramparts

PERSEVERANCE

Sun Shower on tripod ready for showers

John R. Richardson

Filtering water from a spring along the Mackenzie

PERSEVERANCE

Resting along a muddy channel in the Mackenzie Delta

Jackfish Creek cabin

Dan in the community greenhouse in Inuvik

PERSEVERANCE

John in the plane on the way to Tuktoyaktuk

John departing the plane in Tuktoyaktuk

John R. Richardson

Welcome to Tuktoyaktuk – Dan, Don, Phil and John

Dan in front of the Anglican Church in Tuktoyaktuk

PERSEVERANCE

John wading in the frigid Arctic Ocean

John, Dan and Don flexing muscles while wading in the Arctic Ocean

PERSEVERANCE

Fish hanging in a smokehouse in Tuktoyaktuk

Photos of pingos on the horizon taken from the plane

Back to Washington State

THIRTY-ONE
Leaving the Arctic

"A great accomplishment shouldn't be the end of the road, just the starting point for the next leap forward." – Harvey Mackay (American businessman, author and syndicated columnist)

Sunday, July 16, 2006 – Inuvik, Dawson City, and Home

By 5:00 a.m. we were up and packing for our drive down the Dempster Highway. It had rained overnight, and our tent flies were soaked, but they had kept us dry. Much of our gear was already in the truck under the canopy, so it didn't take long to load up.

Before we departed, we walked across the road and had coffee and hot chocolate, compliments of Walter. He and his entourage were up early since they were also leaving Inuvik.

At 6:30 a.m. we turned from the streets of Inuvik onto the Dempster Highway. The distance to Dawson City was approximately 485 mi (781 km), but we were uncertain of the road conditions because of the rain overnight. Knowing it consisted almost entirely of gravel, I wondered if we would be facing a highway similar to the Alcan on my first trip to Alaska.

In 1968, Sue and I moved to Fairbanks in our 1957 Nash Rambler station wagon, driving up the Alaska Highway, which was unpaved almost the entire way. The highway had a number of straight stretches but also had a lot of sharp twists and turns that kept our speed down below 35 mph (56 kph) most of the way. The Alaska Highway, also known as the Alcan Highway, was built during World War II by more than 10,000 American soldiers, providing the first roadway connection between the lower forty-eight states and Alaska. It took less than eight months to complete the crudely constructed road, much of it built over permafrost, tundra, and swampland. It was officially opened in the fall of 1942. In 1968, the road had been improved, but it was still a challenging highway to drive.

The Dempster Highway opened in 1979 after nearly twenty years of construction, environmental impact processes, and other challenges. The Canadians faced environmental challenges similar to those of the Americans who built the Alcan Highway, but they weren't facing the same time constraints. They also had decades of knowledge in the fields of engineering and arctic road construction to rely upon.

I knew the Dempster Highway was built to higher standards than the Alcan, but I wasn't sure of the extent to which road building had progressed in the Arctic. I also wasn't sure of the extent to which the road was maintained. Mother Nature has her own way of keeping us all humble, and I had yet to see how well our Canadian friends were able to meet her challenges.

We estimated it would take about ten hours to reach Dawson City if we kept our average speed at 50 mph (80 kph). If we could maintain that speed, I determined we should arrive in Dawson City at approximately 4:30 p.m.

Our first 80 mi (129 km) of road was smooth, and I was able to keep my speed slightly over 50 mph (80 kph) most of the way. When we reached the ferry landing on the north side of the Mackenzie River across from Tsiigehtchic, the ferry was just landing. It wasn't long before we were on the MV *Louis Cardinal* and crossing the Mackenzie to the landing just to our right of the Arctic Red River. From the ferry landing, the road stretched uphill, and after about 36 mi (58 km) it brought us to the edge of Fort McPherson. Situated along the Peel River, Fort McPherson has a population of approximately 800 people. The wall tent we stayed in the day we crossed the Arctic Circle was made in Fort McPherson by the McPherson Tent and Canvas Company. We drove off the highway and into town, hoping to visit the factory. However, as we suspected, it was closed on Sundays.

Nine miles (14.5 km) past Fort McPherson, we reached the ferry crossing at the Peel River. There was no fee to take any of the three ferries we traveled on in the Northwest Territories. One hundred seventy miles (274 km) past the ferry, we reached a small community, Eagle Plains, that provided services to travelers. We stopped for lunch at a small restaurant/hotel/service station. A vehicle with a trailer carrying a double-ended rowboat was parked nearby. The driver saw the canoes on top of my truck and came over to ask where we had been canoeing. We told him about our adventure, and he explained that he lived in Haines, AK, and would be rowing his boat alone out to an island in the Arctic Ocean. He was a small but rugged sort who seemed more than capable of handling the adventure. I asked him if he knew David Long, who also lived in Haines. David's father, John, is a close friend of mine and was my principal and mentor when I was doing my principal internship in the 1970s. He said he knew David well.

The scenery along the highway became more spectacular as we left Eagle Plains. Wildflowers and low shrubs covered the rolling hills, but there were no trees within our expansive view. Along the shoulders of the road were thickets of low-lying bright pink fireweed plants as far as I could see down the highway. Lakes and meandering streams glistened, reflecting rays of sunlight that broke through the cumulus clouds.

We arrived in Dawson City at 7:20 p.m. and found out the only tent camping was at the Yukon River Government Campground across the Yukon River from the city. The campground was familiar to Dan, Phil, and me because we had camped there on our Yukon River trip. We drove onto another free ferry and set up our tents in sites on the edge of the river.

After dinner we walked onto the ferry and then walked through town to Diamond Tooth Gertie's Gambling Hall to watch the cancan show and partake in liquid refreshments. Don and I got into a friendly political discussion with one another that our cute young waitress apparently didn't think was friendly. I think she swapped tables, because the rest of the night our waitress wasn't so cute or young but looked able to carry out Don under one arm and me under the other. After the show we walked back in time to catch the ferry to the campground, then went to bed.

The next day on our way to Whitehorse, we stopped at a viewpoint and walked down a trail to a platform just above Five Finger Rapids. Five years previously, Phil paddled his kayak, and Dan and I canoed through those roaring rapids, taking on several gallons of water as we raced over large white-topped waves between steep rock outcroppings. It was an experience we will never forget.

We were all anxious to return home to our families, and we traveled long days, only stopping to sleep and eat with one exception, a short hike out to the Liard Hot Springs for a soothing dip in the natural pool, testing our endurance as we slowly worked our way from the cooler end at around 108°F (42°C) to the hotter end at around 126°F (52°C).

In Cliff Jacobson's book, Expedition Canoeing, *he devotes an entire chapter to "Picking a Crew." He writes, "Foremost in selecting a crew is compatibility. All other factors – paddling, skill, age, physical abilities, woodsmanship, and so on—take a back seat to this requirement." He goes on to say, "A canoe crew has an investment in the safety, joy and well-being of all its members. There's no room for loners or egomaniacs."*

I did a great deal of reflecting throughout this expedition but no more so than I did after its completion. Months of planning, 4,100 mi (5,500 km) and 80 hours of traveling in a truck, four long weeks of paddling over 900 mi (1,450 km) for nearly a month, and all the challenges including high water, rough water, and insect bites tested our level of compatibility. I believe we not only passed that test but surpassed what Cliff Jacobson outlined as a compatible crew.

We were able to make decisions without discord, found joy in one another and the people we met, assured each other's safety, and generally had a great time each and every day. We were each very different individuals, but we shared a common goal and a common respect for one another. The bond we created during that long trek is something we will carry for the remainder of our lives. We may have been old geezers, taking on a challenge that even young men would find daunting, but we prevailed and have wonderful stories to tell our families and friends.

Numerous writers of western novels have used the following compliment to honor those frontiersmen who were the toughest and most courageous: "That's a man to ride the river with." I salute our crew by saying, "You are men to ride the river with." And we did just that!

Author's Notes

I made several attempts to start writing this book within the first year or two following the expedition. Because of work, family issues, construction of my cabin on a remote island in British Columbia, and plain old procrastination, I made almost no progress until the end of 2017. When I retired for good, and the cabin was nearly finished, I finally found the fortitude to stick with it. I have written several articles for professional journals and newspapers but nothing more than a few pages long. I hope you found this book interesting and were able to enjoy learning about the amazing Mackenzie River, its history, and the remarkable people who live along it.

I spent many hours trying to decide on a title for the book. In the fall of 2018, I attended a gathering to meet a candidate who had entered a race for the Washington State Senate, Emily Randall. I first met Emily when she entered kindergarten at the school where I spent twenty-three years as principal. When I arrived at the political gathering, Emily gave me a hug and reminded me of one of the strategies I used to enhance my students' vocabulary. The vocabulary word she most remembered was "perseverance." Immediately, I knew the name of my book. As it turned out, Emily (a Democrat) replaced a long-term Republican in my district and became my state senator in January of 2019.

The following is an effort to update readers on some of the people who were mentioned in the book. I searched for information about many of those we met on the river but was able to learn about only those listed below.

- My granddaughter, Caitlyn Richardson, who was born prematurely and spent weeks in the hospital shortly before my departure, is now fourteen years old, healthy, athletic, and nearly as tall as me.
- Jack Kruger was the person we met at the Coast Guard station in Hay River. He kept track of us during the expedition when we checked in with the RCMP either personally or by telephone at the villages and towns along the river. He was then notified by the RCMP of our progress

along the route. Jack had retired from the RCMP in 2003 but continued to work with the RCMP and the Coast Guard, heading up search-and-rescue missions. Jack passed away unexpectedly in June 2014.
- I gave Robert Hardesy my e-mail address when we left Willowlake River. He let me know he received the powdered eggs that Don sent him. He now lives in Fort Simpson and works for the housing authority. He informed me that he and Rita Betsedea were no longer together. Victor Pauncha-Boot was eighty-nine years old when we met him at his home on the river. Unfortunately, Victor passed away the following spring. In December 2018, Robert informed me that Rita had passed away that fall.
- We met Wilfred McDonald at Oscar Creek at the request of his niece, Lisa McDonald, when we were in Norman Wells. Wilfred passed away in October 2013. His family prepared a video to commemorate his life alone on the Mackenzie. You can see the video on YouTube here: https://www.youtube.com/watch?v=d-cilOONxRg
- I was able to contact Lisa McDonald in March of 2020 and she is still living an active life in Norman Wells. Georgie McKay is also still living in Norman Wells but is no longer working for NTCL. I learned from Lisa and Georgie that two of those we met at the Canada Day party have passed away but Storm and the others are still living in Norman Wells.
- Keith Hickling has retired from Fish and Wildlife. He serves on the board of the Sahtu Renewable Resources Board and is working in the oil industry. He has homes in Norman Wells and in Alberta.
- The Northern Transportation Company Limited (NTCL) is the company that transported my truck from Hay River to Inuvik. They provided barge service to Norman Wells, Inuvik, and Tuktoyaktuk as well as other locations along the river. The company filed for bankruptcy in 2016, and its assets were acquired by the Northwest Territories government. The barge service now goes by the name Marine Transportation Service.

APPENDIX A
Mackenzie River Mile Guide

I prepared the following document during the planning stage of this expedition. I searched hundreds of websites as well as printed material to provide a guideline to use in conjunction with topographical maps. Elizabeth Noel's book, *Reflections on a River*, provided a great deal of information that is referenced in the mile guide and in other parts of this book.

I did my best to include information that would make our journey as safe, informative, and as enjoyable as possible. This mile guide was developed for our 2006 trip, so the river, locations, and services have likely changed in the past fourteen years. The distances shown in the mile guide may not be consistent with distances indicated at the end of each chapter due to the way we traveled on the river, changes in the river, and inaccurate estimates. If you are planning a canoe or kayak trip down the Mackenzie, you are welcome to use this as a guideline, but I encourage you to update it with more current information.

John R. Richardson

Disclaimer: The information contained in the Mile Guide was compiled in 2006 for the express purpose of providing a guideline for the 2006 expedition. The Mackenzie River, like all rivers, changes from season to season and from year to year. Services in towns and villages also change. During our expedition, we found that some stores mentioned in the mile guide no longer existed. We also found that RCMP officers were no longer stationed in some of the villages. It is imperative that river travelers do their own research and update the mile guide if they plan to use it for their own expedition.

MILE	GUIDELINES
	Mackenzie River **General Information:** The Mackenzie is the largest river in Canada and the second-largest river in North America, second only to the Mississippi.

0	**Fort Providence**
	    Location: 62°21'N 117°39'W, 3 mi (4.8 km) off the Mackenzie Highway – on a raised clay and sand terrace, surrounded by swamp and muskeg.
	    Population: Approximately 753; Median Age: 30.7; Aboriginal: 675; Religion: 595 Catholic
	    Economy: Tourism, highway rest stop, trapping, Déné handicrafts, firefighting
	    Other: Telephone: NorthwesTel
	The RCMP provides police services.
	Airport with flights to Hay River and Yellowknife
	Free ferry service linking the Mackenzie Highway, operated by the community over the Mackenzie during the summer near Fort Providence
	    Ice road in the location of the ferry during the winter across the Mackenzie River

MILE	GUIDELINES

	History: The first community of "Providence" was located on the north arm of Great Slave Lake. Another "Providence," called Old Fort Providence, was located on Big Island, about 60 mi (96.5 km) upriver from Fort Providence. The present site was founded by missionaries in the mid-1800s with an orphanage and a mission begun by nuns in 1859.
	    In 1928, 600 Déné died during a flu epidemic.
	    In 1970, Queen Elizabeth II came to Fort Providence to start a canoe race to Inuvik.

14.3	**Unnamed Island at Beginning of Mills Lake** **Location**: N61°26'59.6" W118°00'26.5" This is Noel Camp #12, where they stayed on July 10. They found a campsite that had been used before at the east end (upriver end) of the island.
14.0 to 34.0	**Mills Lake** **Location:** Approximately 20 mi (32 km) long and 10 mi (16 km) wide. Travel down the south shore of the lake. Watch for winds that can come up quickly.
28.8	**Big Point** **Location**: N61°23'09" W118°24'12" – on the north shore of Mills Lake where it begins to narrow down

39.3	**Axe Point**
	    Location: N61°17'45" W118°40'45" – on the south shore of the Mackenzie across from White Man's Point
	    An old winter road comes from the Mackenzie Highway to Axe Point and across the river.

MILE	GUIDELINES
41.3	**Noel Camp #13** **Location**: N61°17'50.4" W118°45'12.4" At a small creek with "odd blackish" water. The Noels swam in the creek and found the water unusually warm.
44.3	**Axe Creek** **Location**: N61°51'38.6" W118°47'35.7" On the south side of the river just before a grassy island just offshore
52.4	**Bouvier River** **Location**: N61°13'58" W119°02'10" On the south side of the river. Just offshore is a small island or gravel bar that is sometimes exposed.
58.1	**Wallace Creek** **Location**: N61°13'01" W119°16'41" On the south side of the river
59.3	**Hair Stand Creek** **Location**: N61°13'53" W119°17'31" On the north side of the river
62.3	**Redknife River** **Location**: N61°13'31" W119°22'08" On the south side of the river
66.9	**Small Creek** **Location**: N61°12'57" W119°27'45" On the south side of the river
70.9	**Noel Camp #14** **Location**: N61°15'35" W119°35'35" The Noels said this was not a good site—enough room for two tents only and too close to the water. They stayed there because they were blown off the river. They were concerned that if the river rose during the night, they would be in water.

MILE	GUIDELINES
73.2	**Morrisey Creek** **Location**: N61°16'15" W119°37'58" On the south side of the river
78.6	**Brownings Landing** **Location**: N61°17'46" W119°47'58" On the south side of the river Sandy beach, old cabins in a meadow, lots of strawberry and raspberry bushes. Log cabin that may be inhabited, another log cabin in the process of being built, old horse-drawn farm equipment around. Likely an excellent place to camp.
87.1	**Unnamed Island – east (upriver) end** **Location**: N61°20'41" W119°59'53" The river narrows at this point from 1.5 mi (2.4 km) wide to less than 0.75 mi (1.2 km) wide.
90.3	**Cache Island – east (upriver) end** **Location**: N61°22'40" W120°04'56"
113.3	**Jean Marie River** **Location**: N61°31'39" W120°37'34" **Population**: Approximately 50; Median Age: 39.5; Aboriginal: 45; Religion: 45 Catholic **Economy**: Hunting, fishing, trapping, Déné handicrafts, community sawmill **Other**: Telephone: NorthwesTel, Small store – Go to manager's house since the store is not always open during the day. Only septic is at the school and teacher's home. RCMP come from Fort Simpson. Airstrip – Chartered aircraft is the only air service to the community. Barge service provided from Fort Simpson and Hay River in the summer.

MILE	GUIDELINES
	In winter, is connected to the Mackenzie Highway. Medical provided by visiting doctors and nurses from Fort Simpson.
116.3	**Spence River – Noel Camp #15** **Location**: N61°34'44" W120°40'48" Good camp spot at the bottom of the hill with a firepit and a wooden table The main camp was on a hill—a two-story log building and several smaller cabins with bunk beds and two two-seater outhouses. Raspberry bushes Fish in the river. Noels saw them jumping but couldn't catch any. Beautiful campsite!
130.1	**Rabbitskin River** **Location:** N61°46'55" W120°41'49" Lots of raspberries and blueberries (Saskatoon berries) Old cabin and a few other small old buildings around Beautiful location
133.9	**Strong Point** **Location**: N61°48'54" W120°47'25"
137.9	**Hanson Island** **Location**: N61°41'42" W120°56'07" (east end) This island is about 2 mi (3.2 km) long and is on the left (south) side of the river. The island is close to the mainland and may not look like an island from the river
139.5	**Green Island** **Location**: N61°50'07" W120°57'32" (east end) This island is across from Hanson Island on the right (north) side of the river and is about one third the size.

MILE	GUIDELINES
147.1	**Martin Island** **Location**: N61°51'11" W121°13'52" (east end) This island is in the middle of the river just before Liard River and Fort Simpson. Pass on the left side if stopping at Fort Simpson.
150.9	**Liard River** **Location**: N61°51'03" W121°17'12" (south side of river) This point is where Liard River meets the Mackenzie. Liard River is about 1.5 mi (2.4 km) wide where it enters the Mackenzie. Truesdell Island is at the mouth of the Liard.
153.4	**Fort Simpson** **Location:** N. 61°51'49" W121°20'57" (south side of river) **Population**: Approximately 1,163; Median Age: 31.2; Aboriginal: 795; Religion: 650 Catholic, 230 Protestant **Economy**: Government, transportation, tourism, trapping, local businesses and services, logging, sawmill, traditional activities **Other**: Telephone: NorthwesTel, Departure point for Nahanni National Park Historical center Camping Mackenzie River cruises Arts and crafts RCMP and one bylaw officer Two airports (one territorial and one municipal) with flights connected to Yellowknife One doctor and limited number of nurses Lots of services, including KFC and pizza

MILE	GUIDELINES
	History: Began as a community in 1803 as "Fort of the Forks" and was a fur-trading site. In 1882 it became a permanent settlement when the Hudson's Bay Company started a trading post and named it after George Simpson, the governor of Rupert's Land. The Déné call it Liidli Kue, meaning "The Place Where the Rivers Come Together." Only eight buildings built before 1940 still exist.
160.6	**Martin River – Noel Camp #16** **Location**: N61°55'34.3" W121 34'39.7" (south side of river) There is an area to camp beside a cabin that is occupied. The locals fish for grayling along a one-lane bridge that crosses the Martin River on Highway 1, about a mile south of the Mackenzie.
181.6	**Unnamed Islands mid-river (mile shown is east end of first island)** **Location**: N62°03'47" W122°05'35" From the map, it looks like you can pass on either side.
185.3	**Trail River** **Location**: N62°05'38" W122°12'02" (north side of river—right side)

MILE	GUIDELINES
196.9	**Nduleh (Wrigley) Ferry Crossing** **Location**: N62°08'49" W122°31'41" **Other**: This ferry crossing connects Heritage Highway 1 of the Northwest Territories Highway System. The ferry crossing takes vehicles from the south shore of the Mackenzie to the north shore on a barge pushed by a tug. This highway is a continuation of the Mackenzie Highway that passes through Fort Simpson. From Fort Simpson, it becomes gravel and continues to Wrigley. During the winter the road continues as a winter road from Wrigley through Tulita (Fort Norman), Norman Wells, Fort Good Hope, and to Colville Lake. The ferry operates from 9 a.m. to 11 a.m. and from 2 p.m. to 8 p.m. There is no regular schedule of crossings, providing service as requested. During the winter months, the ferry is closed, and when the ice on the river is thick enough, vehicles cross on the ice. The ferry generally operates from late May through the end of October, depending on the weather. The ice road is used from December through the end of April. The NWT Transportation Department keeps data on the opening and closing of the ice bridge and the start and finish of ferry service each year. This information can be found at http://www.gov.nt.ca/Transportation/hwyinfo/crossing/hwy1-2.htm.
197.7	**Noel Camp #17** **Location**: N62°08'58" W122°31'59" – Just beyond the Nduleh (Wrigley) ferry crossing
198.1	**Unnamed Island** **Location**: N62°09'16" W122°33'16" (east end of island) – 1.25 mi (2 km) past the ferry crossing **Other**: From this point, the river is dotted with numerous islands for almost 70 mi (112.6 km).
225.3	**North Nahanni River** **Location**: N62°15'03" W123°19'39"

MILE	GUIDELINES
225.9	**Noel Camp #18** **Location**: N62°15'18" W123°20'16" **Other**: Good campsite
228.5	**Camsell Bend** **Location**: N63°17'02" W123°22'19" **Other**: At this point the MacKenzie River turns and continues in a more northerly direction toward the Arctic Ocean. From Camsell Bend, stay on the right side of the river, passing the two islands just past the bend.
237.9	**Root River** **Location**: N62°26'13" W123°18'12" (left side of river)
245.3	**McGern Island** **Location**: N62°32'43" W123°13'59" **Other**: McGern Island is 13 mi (21 km) long. Pass on the right side of the island, and travel along the right shore of the river in order to travel by Willowlake River.
256.9	**Willowlake River** **Location**: N62°41'50" W123°07'51" (right side) **Other**: A little more than a mile up the Willowlake River is a bridge on Heritage Highway 1 that is the longest in the Northwest Territories. The Willowlake river was used by the Aboriginal people of the region to bring furs to Fort Alexander. Then the furs were transported on the MacKenzie River. Fort Alexander was a trading post operated by the Northwest Trading Company from 1817 to 1821.

MILE	GUIDELINES
273.9	**River Between Two Mountains** **Location**: N62°56'09" W123°12'48" **Other**: This river comes through the McConnell Range. It has an important cultural history to the Aboriginal people of the area.
274.4	**Noel Camp #19** **Location**: N62°56'37" W123°13'16" – Located just north of the mouth of the River Between Two Mountains **Other**: Nice sandy area for a camp. There's a cabin up on the bank, and when the Noels stopped there in the summer of 1998, an older gentleman who didn't speak English was living in the cabin.
277.9	**Old Fort Island** **Location**: N62°58'4" W123°14'13" (south end) **Other**: The Slavey Déné had a settlement on the island after Fort Alexander closed in 1821.
285.9	**Fish Trap Creek** **Location**: N63°06'16" W123°18'24"
295.3	**Wrigley (Pedzeh Ki)** **Location**: N63°13'35" W123°28'30" **Other**: Wrigley sits on a terrace in a hilly area along the Mackenzie River. It has a population of approximately 168 people, 164 of whom are Aboriginal. The vast majority identify as Catholic and speak South Slavey. The major activities in the area are hunting, fishing, and trapping. Telephone: NorthwesTel—phone located in the hotel A one-man RCMP detachment is located in Wrigley. An airport provides scheduled air service from Fort Simpson. School, one hotel, community health station, co-op store, government gas station, campsite

MILE	GUIDELINES
	The community of Wrigley began between 1900 and 1905 at Fort Wrigley when the Déné migrated from the Hudson's Bay trading post on Old Fort Island after 101 Déné died from famine and tuberculosis. The settlement moved to Hodgson Creek in 1965, a site that was not as wet, so living conditions could be improved. The Noels found the people to be very friendly.
299.3	**Wrigley River** **Location**: N63°14'36" W123°35'14" (left side of river)
314.9	**Ochre River** **Location**: N63°14'36" W123°35'14"
315.5	**Noel Camp #20** **Location**: N63°27'51" W123°41'59" **Other**: The Noels found the beach quite rocky, but there was a flat sandy area about 300 ft (91 m) from the river where they camped.
317.1	**White Sand Creek** **Location**: N63°32'00" W123°44'23" (right side of river) **Other**: The river is quite narrow here; less than a mile wide.
332.4	**Johnson River** **Location**: N63°42'58" W123°54'34" (left side of river)
349.5	**Blackwater River** **Location**: N63°56'31" W124°10'40" (right side of river)
358.7	**Dahadinni River** **Location**: N63°59'09" W124°22'08" (left side of river)
371.3	**Birch Island** **Location**: N64°09'11" W124°25'20"

MILE	GUIDELINES
375.0	**Noel Camp #21** **Location**: N64°13'07 W124°26'40" **Other**: The Noels faced a wall of water about 6 ft (1.8 m) high coming upriver at them broadside shortly after leaving this site. They never did find out why. Keep a lookout!
380.4	**Redstone River** **Location**: N64°17'20" W124°32'27" (left side of river) **Other**: The Noels found lots of neat rocks at this location, where they had stopped to pump water.
386.0	**Saline Island** **Location**: N64°18'45" W124°40'39"
393.5	**Keele River** **Location**: N64°24'44" W124°47'20"
413.6	**Old Fort Point – Noel Camp #22** **Location**: N64°41'12" W124°53'35"
424.1	**Seagull Island** **Location**: N64°44'03" W125°05'26"
434.3	**Police Island** **Location**: N64°51'55" W125°09'18" (northeast tip—middle of the river bend)
447.6	**Fort Norman (Tulita)** **Location**: N64°53'51" W125 33'15" (right side of river) **Other**: The community of Tulita had a population in 2001 of 473 people; 440 of whom were Aboriginal, and nearly all were Catholic. The name was officially changed to Tulita (Where the Waters Meet) on January 1, 1996. The major activities in the community are hunting, fishing, trapping, oil exploration, and tourism. There are outcroppings of coal in the area, and downriver, the coal has been burning since before Mackenzie's expedition

MILE	GUIDELINES
	There is an airport with flights to and from Norman Wells with North Wright Air. The community health center has two nurses. The Northern Store provides food and supplies to the community **History**: The Northwest Company opened a trading post in 1810. Sir John Franklin used this site as the starting point for his expedition. The community grew up around the trading post. The Noels mentioned that an old Hudson's Bay post made of squared logs remains on the edge of the river. (Check to see if this post is the original Northwest Company post,) The original Anglican church constructed in 1860 remains and is being restored.
448.0	**Great Bear River** **Location**: N64°54'15" W125°36'13" (right side of river) **Other**: The Noels reported that the water flowing into the Mackenzie was a teal green color, like water in the Caribbean but cold.
451.2	**Noel Camp #23** **Location**: N64°54'23" W125°41'26.7"
457.0	**Little Bear River** **Location**: N64°55'08" W125°54'11"
483.9	**Ten Mile Islands** **Location**: N65°09'51" W126°28'07"
494.2	**Norman Wells – Noel Camp #24** **Location**: N65°16'35" W125°48'42" **Other**: Norman Wells has a population of approximately 660. Less than one third of these are Aboriginal people. Unlike most of the other communities along the Mackenzie, there are as many Protestants as Catholics. An ecumenical church serves both groups.

MILE	GUIDELINES
	The major activity in the area is oil drilling and exploration. In addition, services surrounding the oil business, transportation, communication, and tourism are also active in the area. Telephone: NorthwesTel A RCMP detachment is located in Norman Wells. Regular air service connects the area with Calgary, Edmonton, Yellowknife, and Inuvik. The airport is a twenty-minute walk from the center of town. Norman Wells has a post office, three motels, and a Northern Store, but Elizabeth Noel reported prices nearly three times higher than in Yellowknife. Norman Wells is connected to the outside world in the summer by air service and barge service. In the winter months, a winter road connects to Wrigley. Norman Wells has a nursing home, and a visiting doctor provides limited medical services. **History**: Most of the communities along the Mackenzie River were established as fur-trading posts. Norman Wells is unique in that it began not around the fur trade but around the oil industry. Alexander Mackenzie observed yellow oil seeping out of the layers of earth along the river in 1789. Long before Mackenzie's expedition, the Déné named the area "Le Gohlini," meaning "where the oil is" (from the Norman Wells website: www.normanwells.com/visit/proud_history.html) In the early 1900s, claims were filed, and eventually, Imperial Oil purchased the claims and began drilling in 1919. A refinery was constructed shortly thereafter, and for nearly fifty years, communities were supplied with its oil.

MILE	GUIDELINES
	During World War II, the United States government commissioned the US Army to quickly construct a pipeline from Norman Wells to Whitehorse. The pipeline's route was known as the Canol Trail and operated from 1944 to 1947. The expense of the operation combined with the end of the war brought an end to the project, and the pipeline was soon dismantled. Another pipeline was later constructed, sending oil from Norman Wells to Zama, Alberta. The oil fields in Norman Wells produce an average of 10 million barrels per year. This oil field is Canada's fourth-largest producing field. Production is expected to continue until at least 2020. Much of the Norman Wells oil field is under the Mackenzie River, so six manmade islands were created to pump oil from beneath the river year round.
503.0	**Rader Island** **Location**: N65°18'09" W127°04'20" **Other**: Pass on the right side.
514.6	**Ogilvie Island** **Location**: N65°24'21" W127°25'08" **Other**: Pass on the left side.
516.5	**Noel Camp #25 on Ogilvie Island** **Location**: N65°25'11" W127°28'26" **Other**: Great camping spot Just beyond Ogilvie Island are several other islands. Judith Island is directly after Ogilvie and is connected when the water is low. After Judith Island, pass to the right of Stanley Island, Willard Island, and Patricia Island.
516.9	**Oscar Creek** **Location**: N65°26'3" W127°27'16.6"

MILE	GUIDELINES
539.1	**Svenson Shoals** **Location**: N65°36'22" W128°03'04" (first shoal) N65°36'35" W128°05'09" (second shoal) **Other**: Pass on the right side. The Carcajou Ridge runs along the north (right) shore of the river.
553.9	**Axel Island** **Location**: N65°37'24" W128°34'22" **Other**: The river widens just before Axel Island. Pass on either side of the island, but the left side should be shorter.
557.7	**Carcajou River** **Location**: N65°37'36" W128°42'27" (left (SW) side of river) **Other**: The outlet to the river is behind an unnamed island on the left of Axel Island.
561.9	**Noel Camp #26** **Location**: N65°40'22" W128°49'00" (left side of river) **Other**: This camp is just before Mountain River and the Sans Sault Rapids. A couple of deteriorating cabins are nearby. The Noels could hear the roar of the rapids from their campsite.
562.8	**Mountain River** **Location**: N65°41'14" W128°49'38" (left side of river) **Other**: From three lakes more than 150 mi (241 km) upstream, canoeists paddle down Mountain River to Fort Good Hope, traversing treacherous rapids and deep canyons. The only access to these three lakes is by floatplane.

MILE	GUIDELINES
562.2	**Sans Sault Rapids** **Location**: N65°41'59" W128°49'22" **Other**: The Noels were told to pass on the left side of the marked channel to avoid the most turbulence. They followed this route and didn't experience even a ripple. The rapids are formed by a rocky ledge that extends from the north (right) shore of the river to about midstream. A sign is posted to warn boaters of the rapids and to stay to the left to avoid the extreme rapids. One website told of a metal teepee with a logbook for river travelers to sign. The logbook was in bad shape in 1998 and may not be there now.
563.4	**Dummit Islands** **Location**: N65°43'12" W128°47'64" **Other**: Pass on left side of island.
572.9	**Hardie Island** **Location**: N65°49'03" W128°54'01"
599.9	**Spruce Island** **Location**: N66°08'20," W129°05'24"
602.4	**Ramparts River** **Location**: N66°10'50," W129°02'24"

MILE	GUIDELINES
604.3	**The Ramparts (Rapids)** **Location:** N66°11'31" W128°55'02" **Other:** Known as "Fee Yee" in Salvey. The legend of its formation is as follows: The Ramparts rapids (located at the head of the Ramparts) were created when Wichididelle threw rocks at a giant beaver. There's also a place where he laid down for a nap—his head and footprints can still be seen today. The small waterfall is where he had a pee. These places are close (to Fort Good Hope). There's a fish camp with cliffs close by where he took a bear. He continued his travels until he got to Bear River, where he killed some beavers and pegged their skins on Bear Rock. His arrows can still be seen in the river near Tulita. They'll remain this way until the end of time. His boat is located above the rapids (Spruce Island is said to be his overturned boat). He said in the legends that he would return one day for it. The giant did return for his boat once but he met the wolverine and told him his intentions to return to this land to get his boat and also that there should be more people for him to eat. The wolverine told him, "Everything remains the same as when he left, not many people there at all." So, the giant turned back and forgot his plans to come back. His boat is still there. (Taken from http://pwnhc.learnnet.nt.ca/research/Places/feeyee.html.) The river narrows down to less than half a mile (0.8 km) at the beginning of the rapids with high limestone cliffs 180 to 300 ft (55 to 91 m) high on either side. The river is nearly 360 ft (110 m) deep through the Ramparts. Mackenzie had been warned of the rapids by the natives in the area. (Mackenzie's journal discusses this.) The general recommendations are to enter the rapids on the right side. There is good fossil hunting along the Ramparts. The Ramparts stretch approximately 7 mi (11 km) and end at Fort Good Hope.

MILE	GUIDELINES
	Mackenzie was warned by the natives that a serpent lived in the water where the river narrows at the beginning of the Ramparts. At the end of the Ramparts, in a small niche high up the cliff wall, stood a statue of the Virgin Mary. Natives in Fort Good Hope told us that it was placed there to protect the villagers from drowning; however, the carver drowned while hunting soon after the statue was completed! But since then nobody has drowned, so it is believed that the Virgin is protecting the people. (http://pages.videotron.com/mousseau/#ramparts).
612.2	**Manitou Island** **Location**: N66°14'51" W128°42'41"
613.5	**Fort Good Hope (Radelih Koe)** **Location**: N66°15'01" W128°38'52" (27 mi (43.5 km) below the Arctic Circle) **Population**: approximately 549; Median Age: 25.4; Aboriginal: 505; Religion: 495 Catholic, 40 Protestant **Economy**: Trapping, hunting, domestic fishing, oil exploration **Other**: Telephone: NorthwesTel Four RCMP officers Three nurses, doctor visits once a month **History**: Fort Good Hope is the oldest settlement in the lower Mackenzie River Valley. It was originally established in 1805 by the Northwest Company but was moved several times. In 1839, the present location was established. In 1859, Father Grollier opened a Roman Catholic mission. Construction of Our Lady of Hope Church began in 1865 and was completed in 1885. Father Emile Petitot came to the parish during its construction and began painting murals on the walls. Other artists from the area added their work to the church. It became a historic site in 1978.

MILE	GUIDELINES
636.6	**Arctic Circle** **Location**: N66°33' **Other**: "The Arctic Circle is the invisible circle of latitude on the earth's surface at 66°33' north, marking the southern limit of the area where the sun does not rise on the winter solstice or set on the summer solstice—a geographic ring crowning the globe. It is approximately 1,650 miles from the North Pole. The Arctic Circle is also the outermost parallel circle counted from the North Pole where we cannot see the sun rise over the horizon in the winter solstice. This phenomenon is called polar night, or midwinter darkness, and occurs around December 21. Continuous day or night ranges from one day at the Arctic Circle to six months at the North Pole." (From http://fairbanks-alaska.com/arctic-circle.htm)
649.8	**Tieda River – Noel Camp #28** **Location**: N66°37'45" W129°20'10" **Other**: The Noels stayed in a cabin at this site. The cabin had a blue tarp on the roof to keep out the rain. An outhouse was nearby. They found lots of high-quality fossils in the area
654.1	**Askew Islands** **Location**: N66°40'11" W129°27'56"
667.9	**Andersons Landing** **Location**: N66°44'14" W129°54'46"
673.3	**Ontaratue River** **Location**: N66°45'38" W130°01'49"
684.9	**Noel Camp #29** **Location**: N66°57'36" W130°9'39" **Other**: Some very old log cabins with sod roofs
696.0	**Bryan Island** **Location**: N67°5'3" W130°13'41"

MILE	GUIDELINES
701.9	**Site of Little Chicago (Right side of river)** **Location:** N67°10'31" W130°13'53" **Other**: Little Chicago was a site used by a group of prospectors headed to the Klondike gold fields. They made their start in Edmonton, intended to travel up the Peel River, over the Ogilvie Mountains, and then to descend down into the gold fields. James A. Michener wrote a book, *The Journey*, that told a story of a team of prospectors who were convinced by unscrupulous profiteers that this would be the shortest and safest route to the gold fields. The real-life prospectors who attempted this route were forced by freezing weather to spend the winter waiting for an attempt the following year. Several were from Chicago, and they named their camp, Little Chicago. They spent that winter trapping and found such success that they stayed for several years following. There is nothing left of the site today.
723.5	**Noel Camp #30 (left side of river)** **Location**: N67°23' 7" W130°52'21" **Other**: On the left side of the river
730.3	**Thunder River (right side of river)** **Location**: N67°28'32" W130°54'36"

MILE	GUIDELINES
740.5	**Travaillant River – Noel Camp #31 - Also known as** *Khaii luk tshik* (Winter Fish at the Mouth) (right side of river) **Location**: N67°27'50," W131°29'30" **Other**: "The mouth of this creek is one of the major trailheads for the route between the Mackenzie River and the large interior lake Khaii luk (Travaillant Lake), an important fish lake for the Gwichya Gwich'in. In the days when schooners were used along the Mackenzie River, Gabe Andre remembers his father taking his schooner out of the river here in the fall using a capstan and storing it over the winter on higher ground up the creek, out of reach of spring ice moving on the Mackenzie River. Dale Clark's father, Wm. (Billy) Clark, was the first person to build a permanent camp here in the late 1920s. He lived here with his family and ran an independent trading post from 1927-1939. People trapping in this area would come and trade here because it was more convenient than travelling to Arctic Red River. Bill McNeely bought Billy Clark's camp in 1942, after selling his camp at Tree River to Hyacinthe Andre. Mr. McNeely ran a trading post at Travaillant Creek from 1942-1956 and then he and his family moved to Fort Good Hope. Bill McNeely's wife Daria was from Arctic Red River. More recently, Maureen Clark of Tsiigehtchic, has been building a frame house here for use by the Clark family as well as travellers and local hunters." (From http://www.gwichin.ca/Research/placeNameMackenzie.asp?num=16)
768.2	**Benoit Creek** (Left side of river) **Location**:
776.1	**Tree River** (left side of river) **Location**:
785.3	**Noel Camp #32** (right side of river) **Location**: N67°12'34" W132°49'16"
788.2	**Adam Cabin Creek** (left side of river) **Location**: N67°12'18" W133°1'32"

MILE	GUIDELINES
802.1	**Pierre Creek (right side of river)** **Location**: N67°19'52" W133°21'14"
814.3	**Start of Lower Ramparts** **Location**: N67°28'1" W133°32'56"

818.9	**Arctic Red River (Tsiigehtchic) (left side of river)**
	Location:
	Other: The town site is located where the Arctic Red River flows into the Mackenzie River. Tsiigehtchic means "Mouth of Iron River." It is believed this name was given because of the red, iron-rich soil in areas up the river from the Mackenzie. The population of Arctic Red River is approximately 195. The Dempster Highway crosses the Mackenzie River at this point. The Mackenzie River and Arctic Red River ferry is free and operates 9:00 a.m. to 12:30 a.m. daily from June to mid-October. Cross by ice bridge in the winter from the end of November until April 30. There is a general store and a community center in the village.
	    Archaeological digs at the mouth of the river indicate that the Gwich'in utilized this excellent fishing eddy centuries before Alexander Mackenzie first gazed up the river in 1789. Elders in the community tell stories of the annual migration up the Arctic Red. Families and bands of people would head upstream once the river level dropped in the late summer. They were heading for the foot of the North Mackenzie Mountains, over 280 km from the mouth of the river. When the flow of the river became too swift for easy upstream travel, they would head overland.
	    Winter camps were established on fishing lakes at the base of the front ranges of the mountains. The people survived the winter by hunting caribou and Dall's sheep and by catching fish through the ice on the lakes. In the spring, they would return to their summer camp at the mouth of the river. Some of the old portage trails can still be found. If one listens carefully, the voices of these travellers can still be heard echoing off the black shale cliffs.

MILE	GUIDELINES
	Today, the river still provides much of the basics of life for the community of Tsiigèhtchic. Dry wood is cut from trees in the white spruce forests for heating homes. In the summer and fall, the river is full of fish nets tended by the residents of Tsiigèhtchic. Hunters return regularly from successful hunts of moose and waterfowl. In the winter, trappers travel hundreds of kilometres upstream to their traditional trapping areas. Sparkling drinking water is melted from large blocks of ice chopped from the river. Missionaries of the Roman Catholic Church first came to Arctic Red River in 1868. The church which graces the mouth of the river was built in 1921. Traders from the Northern Trading Company and the Hudson's Bay Company established rival posts at the river mouth in the 1890s and early 1900s. The RCMP had a detachment here for much of the 20th century. One constable from the Arctic Red River detachment was killed by Albert Johnson, the "Mad Trapper of Rat River." The most significant event in the recent history of the Gwich'in is the settlement of their land claim. Negotiated with the Government of Canada, the Gwich'in Comprehensive Land Claim Agreement gave beneficiaries ownership to large land areas within the Mackenzie Delta and the Arctic Red River region. The agreement also made provisions for Gwich'in involvement in the management of regional natural and cultural resources." (From http://www.chrs.ca/Rivers/ArcticRed/ArcticRed-F_e.htm)

MILE	GUIDELINES
	CROW STORY *(extracted and edited from Annie Norbert's interview on July 8, 1993)* Crow was no good, you know. In the olden days, they say all the animals were human beings, men and women. And Crow liked to fool the people and cheat them too. He got a kick out of it, you know. Sometimes he would scream and make all kinds of noise. Well, I guess he made everybody tired. They couldn't sleep because he made so much noise, especially at night. So, the men grabbed him and took his beak, so that he couldn't talk anymore. They hurt him. He was really suffering; his mouth was sore. He made a plan to get his beak back. He went up the Red [Arctic Red River] not very far from here and made a raft with wood. Then he made people out of moss and placed them on top of it. He picked berries, and he made their eyes too. Then when he was on top of Vik'ooyendik [no translation], he got a little boy to look in his hair for lice. He told that little boy, "Watch for a raft." All of a sudden, that little boy said that a raft was coming. Crow told him that the people on the raft were coming from the mountains. But he fooled the little boy; he lied. They say, Crow is bad to make medicine. Crow told the little boy to go down to the flats and tell everybody that people were coming from up the Red.

MILE	GUIDELINES
	Everybody ran to the bank to meet the people, except for a blind old woman who was looking after Crow's beak. She wanted to go down to the shore too but didn't know where to put the beak. That old woman said, "Gee, I don't know where to put this beak!" That's when Crow lifted up a corner of the tent. "Give it to me!" he said. "Give it to me!" The old woman was blind, so she couldn't see that Crow was speaking. She gave the beak to Crow. Crow put his beak back on so fast that he put it on crooked! That's how Crow fooled the people so he could get his beak back. (See http://www.gwichin.ca/Research/placeNameArcticRed.asp)
822.3	**Noel Camp #33** (left side of river) **Location**: N67°29'2" W133°48'12"
832.9	**Point Separation** (right side of river) **Location**: N67°36'37" W133°05'27" **Other**: Stay to the right shoreline to make sure you can locate the entrance of the East Channel.
847.5	**Entrance to East Channel** (right side of river) **Location**: N67°47'14" W134°11'24" **Other**: Take this entrance and follow the channel to Inuvik.
853.5	**Noel Camp #34** (right side of river) **Other**: Very muddy site. Would not work out well if it's raining or wet
863.4	**Fork in Channel** **Location**: N67°58'27" W134°01'43" **Other**: Stay on the right side of the river, and follow to the right.
884.1	**Sharp Bend in the Channel** **Location**: N68°12'14" W133°48'54"

MILE	GUIDELINES
900.6	**Inuvik – Noel Camp #35 "The Place of Man"** **Location**: N68°21'29" W133°42'44" **Other**: The population of Inuvik is approximately 3,300 citizens, 60 percent non-native. Of the native population, 25 percent are Inuit (Inuvialuit), and 15 percent are Déné/Metis. It sits east of the Richardson Mountains on a flat wooded plateau. Inuvik is 10 degrees farther west than Vancouver. There is one traffic light in the city. The local airport is 8 mi (12.9 km) from the city center. During the summer, there are fifty-six days with twenty-four hours of daylight. Conversely, mostly during the month of December, there are thirty straight days when the sun does not rise. The warmest month is July, and the wettest is August. Inuvik is the last stop on the 456-mi (734-km) unpaved Dempster Highway. During the winter months, it's possible to drive from Inuvik to Tuktoyaktuk over a winter road when the lakes and rivers freeze. During the summer months, travel from Inuvik to Tuk must be by water or air. > Inuvik is Canada's northernmost modern town, located almost 200 mi (321 km) north of the Arctic Circle. It was built by the Canadian government in 1955–1963, largely because the existing town in the area, Aklavik, seemed about to be washed away by the Mackenzie River. Every building in town was built on pilings to prevent melting of the permafrost. Central heat, water, power, and sewage are provided through a system of insulated aboveground "utilidors" connecting all buildings (utilities cannot be buried in the frozen ground). The population of about 3,000 is split more or less evenly between Athabascan Indians (the Déné), Eskimos (Inuit), and other Canadians, many of whom work for the government. (See more here: http://virtualguidebooks.com/NWT/LowerMackenzie/Inuvik/DowntownInuvikL.html)

MILE	GUIDELINES
	Some of the residents of Inuvik decided to turn an old ice rink slated for demolition into a community greenhouse. The Inuvik Community Greenhouse is the most northerly commercial greenhouse operation and the only greenhouse of its kind in Canada. The building houses two areas: raised community garden plots on the main floor and a small commercial greenhouse on a second floor. The garden plots are available to Inuvik residents and some are reserved for Elders and other community groups. The commercial greenhouse produces bedding plants (flowers and starter veggie plants) and also a crop of tomatoes and English cucumbers. (See more here: http://www.cityfarmer.org/inuvik.html.)
908.2	**Fork in Channel** **Location**: N68°26'05" W133°48'50" **Other**: Take the right fork, which should be the larger of the two.
918.6	**Harrison Island on the left entering larger channel** **Location**: N68°33'38" W133°58'46" **Other**: Three channels enter at this location. Continue north; the channel widens here. Harrison Island continues for approximately 7 mi (11.2 km) on the left side.
928.5	**Reindeer Station, Noel Camp #36** **Location**: N68°41'34" W134°11'0" **Other**: The Canadian government established this site in the early 1930s. Reindeer were brought there from Alaska and kept on a 6,600-sq.-mi (17,000-sq.-km) grazing reserve. At one time a Hudson's Bay Company trading post was located there, and a freighter, the *Pelican Rapids*, would stop there. Several buildings exist there today.

MILE	GUIDELINES
	In the early 1900s, wild caribou, which were an important source of food for the Inuvialuit became scarce. The federal government arranged for a herd of domestic reindeer to be brought across from Alaska and encouraged the Inuvialuit to become herders. A base for the new reindeer industry was built on the East Channel of the Mackenzie River. The government name for the base was Reindeer Station, but many Inuvialuit called it Qun'ngilaat. At its peak, Reindeer Station was like a small town with houses, a school, workshops, and warehouses. Reindeer Station was closed in the late 1960s when the base of the reindeer operations was moved to Inuvik. (See more at: http://pwnhc.learnnet.nt.ca/inuvialuit/placenames/qunngilaatexplore.html.) Another source of information on reindeer and Reindeer Station: *The Sami/Inupiaq/Yup'ik Reindeer in Alaska & Canada Story* (including important dates in contemporary Sami history) by Nathan Muus (http://www.baiki.org/content/alaskachron/pre1890.htm).
935.3	**Entering New Channel** **Location**: N68°44'33" W134°18'12"
945.4	**Spruce Island** **Location**: N68°52'49" W134°31'28" **Other**: Pass to the right
948.9	**Lower Island** **Location**: N68°55'34" W134°36'23" **Other**: Pass to the right
954.7	**Tununuk Point – Noel Camp #37 (right side of channel)** **Location**: N68°59'59" W134°40'30" **Other**: This camp spot is on the north side of Neklek Channel, which meets the East Channel we will be following. It has an old airfield and lots of abandoned oil equipment

MILE	GUIDELINES
962.1	**Lucas Point** **Location**: N69°3'36" W134°35'42" **Other**: Located on the right side of the river
968.0	**Swimming Point** **Location**: N69°5'46" W134°23'31" **Other**: Located on the left side of the river
981.1	**Unnamed Island (pass on the right)** **Location**: N69°15'36" W134°6'30"
987.7	**Noel Camp #34 (right side of channel)** **Location**: N69°18'17" W133°54'08"
990.6	**Kittigazuit Bay** This is the beginning of the Arctic Ocean. Stay safely behind the islands and the mainland. There are sandbars that may need to be traversed.
999.7	**Opening of bay near Whitefish Pingo** **Location**: N69°23'22" W133°34'13" **Other**: Whitefish Pingo is marked on the map here, but it does not pinpoint the pingo. This entire area has the largest concentration of pingos in the world with nearly 1,400 on the Tuktoyaktuk Peninsula.
1004.3	**Naparotalik Spit** **Location**: N69°23'30" W133°22'06" **Other**: This spit juts out into the ocean and is between two small bays. The first bay is named Vanyanek Inlet and is the deeper of the two.
1008.4	**Peninsula Point** **Location**: N69°23'58" W133°10'33" **Other**: This point is at the end of a long peninsula that runs parallel to our course. From Google Earth, it looks like there could be protection behind the peninsula if the wind comes up.

MILE	GUIDELINES
1013.9	**Tuktoyaktuk (means "resembling a caribou")** 　　**Location**: N69°27'22" W133°02'20" Located on a spit along the Arctic Ocean. 　　**Population**: Approximately 930; Median Age: 23.9; Aboriginal: 930; Religion: 320 Catholic, 534 Protestant; Education Level: 26.2 percent of people age 20–34 with a high school education, 11.1 percent of people age 35–44 with a high school education, 14.3 percent of people age 45–64 with high school education 　　**Other**: In 1950 Fort Brabant was officially renamed Tuktoyaktuk, the name used by the native people of the area. The north side of the spit has eroded more than 328 ft (100 m) in the past fifty years. Tuktoyaktuk, commonly referred to as Tuk, is the base for oil exploration in the Beaufort Sea. Reindeer herding is one of the activities in this area.

Printed in Canada